Notary Public Guidebook
for North Carolina

Sixth Edition
William A. Campbell

Institute of Government The University of North Carolina at Chapel Hill 1991

THE INSTITUTE OF GOVERNMENT of The University of North Carolina at Chapel Hill is devoted to teaching, research, and consultation in state and local government.

Since 1931 the Institute has conducted schools and short courses for city, county, and state officials. Through monographs, guidebooks, bulletins, and periodicals, the research findings of the Institute are made available to public officials throughout the state.

Each day that the General Assembly is in session, the Institute's *Daily Bulletin* reports on the Assembly's activities for members of the legislature and other state and local officials who need to follow the course of legislation.

Over the years the Institute has served as the research agency for numerous study commissions of the state and local governments.

John L. Sanders, DIRECTOR
William A. Campbell, ASSOCIATE DIRECTOR

FACULTY

Stephen Allred
A. Fleming Bell, II
Frayda S. Bluestein
Joan G. Brannon
Stevens H. Clarke
Ann C. Clontz
Janine M. Crawley
Anne M. Dellinger
James C. Drennan
Richard D. Ducker
Robert L. Farb
Joseph S. Ferrell

S. Grady Fullerton
Milton S. Heath, Jr.
Joseph E. Hunt
Kurt J. Jenne
Robert P. Joyce
Jeffrey S. Koeze
Patricia A. Langelier
David M. Lawrence
Charles D. Liner
Ben F. Loeb, Jr.
Ronald G. Lynch
Janet Mason

Richard R. McMahon
Laurie L. Mesibov
David W. Owens
Robert E. Phay
John Rubin
Roger M. Schwarz
Robert G. Shreve
Michael R. Smith
Mason P. Thomas, Jr.
Thomas H. Thornburg
A. John Vogt

© 1991
Second Printing, 1992
INSTITUTE OF GOVERNMENT
The University of North Carolina at Chapel Hill
⊖ The paper used in this publication meets the minimum requirements
of American National Standard for Information Sciences
Permanence of Paper for Printed Library Materials, ANSI Z39.48-1984.
Printed in the United States of America
I S B N   1-56011-186-0

♺ Printed on recycled paper.

Contents

Contents

Preface

The first edition of the Institute of Government's *Notary Public Guidebook*, by Elmer R. Oettinger and Harry W. McGailliard, was published in 1939; the second edition, by Royal G. Shannonhouse and Willis Clifton Bumgarner, in 1956; the third edition, by Ann H. Phillips, in 1965; and the fourth edition, by J. Ritchie Leonard and Patrice Solberg, in 1977. I wrote the fifth edition, published in 1984, and this sixth edition, which reflects the numerous changes in the laws and practices affecting notaries public since the fifth edition.

Although a notary's commission can be obtained with relative ease, rights of considerable consequence may depend on the correct performance of the notarial function. The notary cannot be expected to discover without help the laws, practices, and forms essential to the office and its performance. This book seeks to furnish that help by weaving law, forms, and practice into a brief, systematic, and convenient reference work, and it should also be of substantial value to registers of deeds, clerks of superior court, and practicing attorneys.

I am grateful for the valuable assistance, always graciously given, of Ludelle R. Hatley, notaries public director in the Department of the Secretary of State, and Faye Senter, staff development specialist, Vehicle Registration Section, Division of Motor Vehicles, in preparing this edition. Their comments and suggestions have improved this guidebook.

Chapel Hill
Fall 1991

I
The Office

Introduction

The office of notary public can be traced to the early Roman Empire. In the seventeenth and eighteenth centuries the notarial function became especially important as merchants and shippers ventured far from local markets, because commercial agreements entered into in distant places required acknowledgment in a manner that would be respected at home.[1] In 1777, the North Carolina General Assembly authorized the Governor to appoint "from time to time . . . one or more persons, properly qualified, to act as notary or notaries at the different ports in this state."[2] The statute was amended in 1799 to allow notaries to be appointed in every North Carolina county.[3] Throughout North Carolina more than 130,000 persons now serve as notaries.[4]

All fifty states have notaries, but their manner of appointment, tenure of office, and powers and duties vary greatly from state to state. A North Carolina notary should never assume that he or she can do what a notary in another state can do; the powers and duties of a North Carolina notary are determined by North Carolina law.

Appointment of Notaries

Power to appoint

Although formerly the governor appointed notaries in North Carolina,[5] current law assigns this power to the secretary of state, with the only

1. For a more detailed history of notaries, see 58 AM. JUR. 2D *Notaries Public* § 2 (1971); ANDERSON'S MANUAL FOR NOTARIES PUBLIC 1-2 (2d ed. 1956); L. Greene, Law of Notaries Public 1 (Legal Almanac Series No. 14, 2d rev. ed. 1967).

2. Laws of N.C., ch. 8, § 15 (1777).

3. *Id.*, ch. 15 (1799).

4. Interview with Notaries Public Director Ludelle Hatley, Department of the Secretary of State, in Raleigh, N.C. Oct. 26, 1990).

5. Laws of N.C., ch. 8, § 15 (1777).

limitation that the appointee meet the qualifications discussed below.[6] The number of notaries appointed in any county or in the entire state is not limited.

Qualifications for office

Both the North Carolina Constitution and the General Statutes impose qualifications for holding the office of notary. Because the office is a public one,[7] the provisions of Article VI, Section 8, of the state constitution apply. This section prohibits any person from holding office who has been (1) convicted of a felony under North Carolina or federal law, (2) convicted in another state of a felony if the crime would also be a felony had it been committed in North Carolina, (3) convicted of corruption or malpractice in any office, or (4) removed from any office by impeachment and not restored to the rights of citizenship as prescribed by law.[8] G.S. 10A-4(b) limits eligibility to persons eighteen years old or older who reside or work in North Carolina.

Under the dual-officeholding provisions of the North Carolina Constitution, a person serving as a notary is expressly authorized to hold concurrently another elective or appointive state or federal office.[9]

Application for appointment

To request the application form for appointment as a notary, a person should either visit the local register of deeds or write to the following address: Notaries Public Director, Department of the Secretary of State, Legislative Office Building, 300 North Salisbury Street, Raleigh, North Carolina 27603-5909. The form requires the applicant to provide and certify the truthfulness of certain personal information, and it must contain no misstatement or omission of fact. An applicant should give his or her full name (no nicknames) on the application. A recommendation is required from a North Carolina elected official, and it must be contained on the application. A register of deeds who is the instructor of the course discussed in the next section may sign the application at the course's conclusion to serve as this required recommendation. The application must be completed

---

6. N.C. GEN. STAT. § 10A-4.

7. *See* N.C. CONST. art. VI, § 9(2).

8. Article VI, Section 8, of the North Carolina Constitution also disqualifies persons for public office who "deny the being of Almighty God," but this disqualification is not enforced because it clearly violates the First Amendment of the United States Constitution. Torcasco v. Watkins, 367 U.S. 488 (1961); 41 N.C. Att'y Gen. Rep. 727 (1972).

9. N.C. CONST. art. VI, § 9(2).

in ink, signed by the applicant, and acknowledged before a person authorized to administer oaths.[10]

The applicant should return the completed application form with the recommendation and a check or money order for the statutory fee of $25.00, payable to the "Secretary of State of North Carolina."[11] This nonrefundable fee is required for the issuance of the commission.[12] The secretary of state's office does not furnish notarial stamps or seals.

The secretary of state may deny an application if the applicant has been convicted of a crime involving moral turpitude or dishonesty; has had a notarial commission or other professional license revoked, suspended, or restricted by North Carolina or another state; or has engaged in official misconduct, whether or not disciplinary action resulted.[13]

Notarial instruction

Before being appointed, applicants must complete a course of instruction in the duties of notaries approved by the secretary of state. This course must contain from three to six hours of classroom instruction.[14] Approved courses are currently offered by all community colleges and technical institutes; the local register of deeds will know where approved courses are taught. Practicing attorneys are exempt from this instructional requirement,[15] but before other applicants will be issued a commission, the secretary of state must have received certification from the educational institution that they have successfully completed the course. These instructional requirements are waived for second and subsequent commissions.[16]

Before they are commissioned, all applicants (including attorneys) must also purchase[17] and retain for reference purposes[18] a manual approved by the secretary of state describing the duties and responsibilities of a notary. This book, the Institute of Government's *Notary Public Guidebook for North Carolina*, is currently the approved manual.

---

10. N.C. GEN. STAT. § 10A-4(b)(5).

11. *Id.* § 10A-7.

12. Hatley, *supra* note 4.

13. N.C. GEN. STAT. § 10A-4(c).

14. *Id.* § 10A-4(b)(3). To complete the notary's course of instruction, an applicant obviously must be literate, and the attorney general has so ruled [letter from N.C. Att'y Gen. to Ludelle Hatley (Jan. 7, 1987)], though literacy is not *statutorily* required.

15. N.C. GEN. STAT. § 10A-4(b)(3).

16. *Id.* § 10A-6.

17. *Id.* § 10A-4(b)(4).

18. *Id.*

Issuance of commission

The notaries public director in the Department of the Secretary of State attempts to verify the information provided in selected applications, and a commission will be denied if the director finds that the applicant has supplied inaccurate information. Unless the application is incomplete or inaccurate or unless an investigation reveals that an applicant is disqualified from serving as a notary, the secretary of state's policy is to issue a commission upon receiving the community college's certification that the applicant has successfully completed the training course.

Formal Induction

The secretary of state's office sends the newly appointed notary's commission, along with a transmittal letter, directly to the register of deeds of the county where the appointee lives or works.[19] A copy of the transmittal letter is sent by the secretary of state to the appointee as official notice that he or she has been named a notary. The appointee must then appear before the local register of deeds to qualify by taking an oath of office. Notaries take the constitutional and statutory oaths prescribed for all public officers,[20] as well as the following oath of office:[21] "I, _____, do swear [or affirm] that I will well and truly execute the duties of the office of notary public according to the best of my skill and ability, according to law, so help me, God."[22] The newly commissioned notary must pay the $5.00 register's fee for administering the oath.[23]

If the appointee does not appear before the register of deeds within ninety days of receiving the transmittal letter, the register returns the commission to the secretary of state, and the applicant must reapply for a commission.[24]

After taking the oath, the notary signs his or her name (exactly as it appears on the commission) in "The Record of Notaries Public" maintained by the register of deeds. This record contains the notary's name and signature, the effective date of the commission, its expiration date, and the date the oath was administered. Should the secretary of state ever re-

---

19. *Id.* § 10A-8.
20. N.C. CONST. art. VI, § 7 and N.C. GEN. STAT. § 11-7.
21. *See* N.C. GEN. STAT. § 10A-8.
22. *See id.* § 11-11 (General Oath).
23. *Id.* § 161-10(a)(17).
24. *Id.* § 10A-8.

voke the commission, the revocation date will also be entered in this record. After the notary signs the book, the register of deeds delivers the notary's commission. The register then completes the certificate of qualification and returns it to the secretary of state. After receiving the certificate, the secretary of state places the appointee's name on the official roll of notaries (kept in the secretary's office).

Although an appointee may take the oath of office at any time after receiving notification of the appointment, he or she may not exercise any powers of office until the effective date of the commission specified in the transmittal letter.[25] Entering upon the duties of the office before taking, subscribing, and filing the oath of office is a criminal offense and constitutes grounds for revoking the commission.[26]

Tenure of Office

Effective period

A notary's commission is valid for the five-year period shown on the commission unless revoked. The term of office begins on and includes the effective date of the commission and ends at midnight on the day preceding the fifth anniversary of the effective date.[27] A notary may qualify by taking the oath at any time during the life of the commission, regardless of whether the secretary of state issuing the commission remains in office. Delay in qualifying, however, does not extend the term of the commission. For example, if the effective date of the commission was June 5, 1990, and the notary did not qualify by taking the oath until July 6, 1991, the commission would expire at midnight on June 4, 1995, not on July 5, 1996.

Renewal

Strictly speaking, notaries' commissions are not renewed. Each so-called renewal is a new appointment, and with each new appointment a notary must qualify again by taking the oath of office before continuing to perform the duties of a notary. The same procedure must be followed as for the first appointment except that the course of instruction need not be taken again. The number of successive appointments that a notary may obtain has no limit.

---

25. 41 N.C. Att'y Gen. Rep. 435 (1972).

26. N.C. GEN. STAT. § 14-229. One who acts officially without taking the oath of office is also subject to a $500 fine. *Id.* § 128-5.

27. *Id.* § 10A-5.

The notary's commission states its expiration date. A notary should not apply for a new appointment until approximately four weeks before the current commission expires. The application, with a check for $25.00, should be sent to the following address: Notaries Public Director, Department of the Secretary of State, Legislative Office Building, 300 North Salisbury Street, Raleigh, North Carolina 27603-5909. The bottom of the transmittal letter informing notaries of their appointments carries a blank application form for the next appointment five years later.

Notaries sometimes mistakenly perform official acts after their commission expires but before they are reappointed and take the oath for another term. This is a criminal offense that can lead to revocation of the notary's commission.[28]

Change of status

Notaries who change their addresses or names or resign their commissions are required to notify the secretary of state.[29] Within thirty days of changing his or her address, a notary must notify the secretary of state by certified or registered mail of the old and new addresses. Within thirty days of changing his or her name, a notary must notify the secretary of state by reapplying for a commission. The secretary then cancels the old commission, issues a commission in the new name, and directs the notary to appear again before the register of deeds for administration of the oaths. A name change and new commission requires the purchase of a new seal. A notary who resigns his or her commission must notify the secretary of state by registered or certified mail, giving the effective date of resignation. A notary who no longer works or lives in North Carolina must resign his or her commission.

Premature termination of commission

A notary's office may be vacated during the term in three ways. First, the notary may submit a voluntary resignation to the secretary of state; his or her name is then removed from the roll of notaries. Second, a court proceeding in the nature of quo warranto can successfully challenge the notary's qualifications. Third, the secretary of state may revoke the commission of any notary against whom a complaint is made if the secretary finds that the notary in performing his or her duties has not complied with state laws.[30]

---

28. *See id.* §§ 14-229 and 10A-12(a).
29. *Id.* § 10A-13.
30. *Id.* § 10A-13(d).

Commissions have most commonly been revoked when notaries have certified documents not acknowledged or proved in their presence. Commissions have also been revoked when notaries have allowed other persons to use their seals. Every complaint concerning the conduct of a notary is examined by the notaries public director, who relies on an investigator in the secretary of state's office. The notary is informed of the complaint's nature by the notaries public director and is invited to respond. If there is a factual dispute between the complainant and the notary, the deputy secretary of state holds a hearing, and the notary may be accompanied by anyone he or she chooses, including an attorney. After the hearing, the deputy secretary of state makes a recommendation to the secretary of state concerning revocation, and, in appropriate cases, the notaries public director informs the district attorney in the county where the notary resides that the notary may have committed a crime. The hearing and judicial-review provisions of the Administrative Procedure Act apply to revocation proceedings.[31]

When the decision to revoke a commission is made, the secretary of state issues a revocation order and mails copies to the notary and to the register of deeds of the notary's county. The order becomes effective two days from the date of the letter; the performance of notarial acts after a commission has been revoked is a criminal offense.[32]

Criminal offenses

The following actions are made crimes by the notary law:
(1) holding oneself out to the public as a notary or performing notarial acts without a commission (misdemeanor);[33]
(2) taking, while a notary, an acknowledgment or performing a verification or proof without personal knowledge or satisfactory evidence of the signer's identity (misdemeanor);[34]
(3) taking, while a notary, an acknowledgment or performing a verification or proof knowing it to be false or fraudulent (class J felony);[35] and
(4) knowingly soliciting or coercing a notary to commit official misconduct (misdemeanor).[36]

---

31. *See* N.C. GEN. STAT. §§ 150B-2(3), -3, and -23.
32. *Id.* § 10A-12(a).
33. *Id.*
34. *Id.* § 10A-12(b).
35. *Id.* § 10A-12(c).
36. N.C. GEN. STAT. § 10A-12(d).

II
General Powers

Scope

A North Carolina notary may perform any of the following notarial acts:

(1) acknowledgments;
(2) oaths and affirmations; and
(3) verifications or proofs.[1]

An *acknowledgment* is an act "in which a notary certifies that a signer, whose identity is personally known to the notary or proven on the basis of satisfactory evidence, has admitted, in the notary's presence, having signed a document voluntarily."[2]

An *oath* or *affirmation* is an act "in which a notary certifies that a person made a vow or affirmation in the presence of the notary, with reference made to a Supreme Being for an oath and with no reference made to a Supreme Being for an affirmation."[3]

A *verification* or *proof* is an act "in which a notary certifies that a signer, whose identity is personally known to the notary or proven on the basis of satisfactory evidence, has, in the notary's presence, voluntarily signed a document and taken an oath or affirmation concerning the document."[4]

Limitations

Territory

A North Carolina notary may act outside his or her home county and may change county of residence during the term of the

---

1. N.C. GEN. STAT. § 10A-9(a).
2. *Id.* § 10A-3(1).
3. *Id.* § 10A-3(5).
4. *Id.* § 10A-3(9).

commission.[5] A notary may also take the acknowledgment or proof of any instrument permitted or required to be registered regardless of the county in this state where the subject matter of the transaction is located, and regardless of the residence, domicile, or citizenship of the persons who sign the instrument or for whose benefit the instrument is made.[6] Like most states,[7] North Carolina does not recognize acts of out-of-state notaries performed within this state.[8] For example, an attestation by a South Carolina notary while visiting in North Carolina is invalid, and so, too, is an official act by a North Carolina notary while in another state.

On the other hand, acts of a notary of another state properly performed within his or her home state are fully recognized insofar as they are within the powers given to notaries by North Carolina law;[9] thus an attestation by a South Carolina notary performed within South Carolina according to South Carolina law is valid in this state. If a notary of another state takes the proof or acknowledgment of an instrument and the instrument does not show the notary's seal or stamp and the expiration date of the notary's commission, then the county official before whom the notary qualified for office must certify that the notary was an acting notary at the time of this certificate and that the notary's signature is genuine. This officer's certificate must be under seal and must accompany the notary's certification of the instrument.[10]

A North Carolina notary may perform within this state, regarding a transaction to be made in another state, any notarial function that (a) is authorized by the law of that state and (b) is to be performed for some purpose that is proper within that state. Also, notaries are frequently authorized to act in cases involving the federal government and federal agencies; the precise nature of this authority is discussed under appropriate headings in this guidebook.[11]

Practice of law

A notary who is not a licensed attorney may not practice law.[12] The practice of law includes the following, whether rendered with or without compensation: preparing or helping to prepare deeds, deeds of

---

5. *Id.* § 10A-5.

6. N.C. GEN. STAT. § 47-6.

7. 1 AM. JUR. 2D *Acknowledgments* § 28 (1962).

8. *See* County Sav. Bank v. Tolbert, 192 N.C. 126, 133 S.E. 558 (1926).

9. N.C. GEN. STAT. §§ 10A-9(d), 47-2.

10. *Id.* § 47-2.2.

11. See Ch. IV, "Federal Law."

12. N.C. GEN. STAT. § 84-4.

trust, mortgages, wills, or similar documents; abstracting or advising on titles to real or personal property; and giving opinions as to the legal rights of any person.[13] However, a notary as a private citizen may prepare deeds or other instruments for a transaction to which he or she is a party,[14] as well as notarial certificates to be executed by him- or herself as notary.

Named party and interested party

A notary is disqualified from performing the duties of the office in any case in which he is a signer of the document or is named in the document, except as a trustee in a deed of trust.[15] Additionally, a notary is disqualified from acting if the notary will receive directly from a transaction connected with the notarial act any commission fee, right, title, interest, cash, property, or other consideration in excess of the notary fees specified in G.S. 10A-10.[16] Fees or other consideration for services rendered by a lawyer, real estate broker or salesman, motor vehicle dealer, or banker are excluded for purposes of determining this disqualification.[17] Thus, essentially, if a notary will receive anything of value from the transaction over and above the notary fees (except for the services listed above), the notary is disqualified.

While many laws have validated the acts of notaries who were interested in transactions,[18] most of these curative laws apply only to past transactions. Thus notaries should not perform official duties when they are "interested" parties to a transaction.

Preparation or probate of wills

A notary who is not also a licensed attorney may not prepare or aid in preparing a will for another person[19] but may witness a will if he or she is a disinterested party.

Only the clerk of the superior court may probate wills.[20] The notary's role in the acknowledgment of ordinary attested wills and in the attestation of self-proved wills is discussed in Chapter IV.

---

13. *Id.* § 84-2.1.
14. *See* State v. Pledger, 257 N.C. 634, 127 S.E.2d 337 (1962).
15. N.C. GEN. STAT. § 10A-9(c)(1).
16. *Id.* § 10A-9(c)(2).
17. *Id.*
18. *Id.* §§ 47-62, -63, -64, -92, -93, -94, -95, -100.
19. *Id.* § 84-4.
20. *Id.* § 31-17.

Performance of marriage

A notary is not authorized to perform a marriage ceremony unless he or she is also an ordained minister or a magistrate.[21]

Judicial functions

While many notarial duties are quasi-judicial, a notary's powers are limited to those specifically granted by statute. Unless also a judicial officer, the notary has no power to issue warrants, summonses, or subpoenas or to try civil or criminal court cases (the power to administer oaths and take affidavits is discussed in Chapters V and VI).

---

21. *Id.* § 51-1.

III
Attestation

Requirements for Attestation

A notary public in North Carolina must attest his official acts by a clear and legible impression of his seal (or stamp), by his proper signature, by the readable appearance of his name, and by a statement of the expiration date of his commission.[1] A notary customarily supplies the date and place of attestation if this information does not appear elsewhere on the writing, but it is not required by statute.

Omission of either the seal or the signature invalidates a notarial act.[2] Although numerous statutes validate the past acts of notaries from which seals were omitted,[3] notaries should not count on a future validation statute to correct their errors.

The seal

The notarial seal symbolizes the power given to the notary by the state. Past practice was to impress seals in wax attached to the paper, but the statute now calls for an impression directly on the document.[4] The presence of the seal on a writing raises a presumption that the writing was attested in the manner required by law by a notary.[5] The notary's seal will not, however, cure a certificate otherwise defective on its face.[6]

---

1. N.C. GEN. STAT. § 10A-9(b).

2. In Tucker v. Interstate Life Ass'n, 112 N.C. 796, 17 S.E. 532 (1893), the court held that an attempted verification of a pleading before a notary was ineffective because the notary did not affix his official seal. The strict necessity for the seal was not changed by Peel v. Corey, 196 N.C. 79, 144 S.E. 559 (1928), although the case is annotated under former North Carolina General Statute 10-9 to suggest that the requirement has been dropped. Presumably, the omission of the notary's signature would, like the omission of the seal, invalidate the notarial act.

3. N.C. GEN. STAT. §§ 47-53, -53.1, -102, -103.

4. See id. § 10A-9(b)(2).

5. See State v. Knight, 169 N.C. 333, 344, 85 S.E. 418, 424 (1915).

6. See McClure v. Crow, 196 N.C. 657, 146 S.E. 713 (1929).

A North Carolina notary may use either a seal or a stamp in attesting official acts[7] (when using a stamp, the notary should be careful to place it on a blank space of the document so that it does not obscure any of the text). The seal or stamp should always be placed on the same page as the notary's signature and close to the signature and expiration date. It must contain the name of the notary exactly as the name appears on the commission, the county in which he or she was appointed and qualified, the words "North Carolina" or an appropriate abbreviation, and the words "Notary Public."[8] The impression must be distinct enough for this information to be reproducible by photographic means. The impression of a seal must be smudged (with carbon or similar material) before it can be reproduced photographically, and a notary must replace the seal when it no longer makes a reproducible impression.[9]

So that the device may be used for more than one term, the secretary of state advises against including the expiration date of the notary's commission on the face of the seal or stamp.

The signature

The notary's signature must be written exactly as it appears on the commission.[10] Thus the name in the seal or stamp and the signature must always match. Any initials used on the commission must be used in the signature. In the signature, no deviation from the name on the commission is acceptable. If a notary changes his or her name, he or she must apply for a new commission pursuant to G.S. 10A-13(f) and purchase a seal with the new name (see Chapter I, "Change of status").

Residence

Although commissioned for a specific county, a North Carolina notary may perform official acts anywhere within the state boundaries.[11] When a notary acts outside his or her home county, the county name in the official seal will not match the county name in the certification. For example, if a Davidson County notary certifies a document in Rowan County, the certification will begin:

---

7. N.C. GEN. STAT. § 10A-11.
8. *Id.*
9. *Id.*
10. *Id.* § 10A-9(b)(1).
11. *Id.* § 10A-5.

```
North Carolina
Rowan County

I, [name of notary], a Notary Public for
said County and State, . . . .
```

The seal on the document will show, however, that the notary is commissioned in Davidson County, not in Rowan. Certificates with this difference are nonetheless valid.

A notary moving to another county during the term of the commission should continue using his or her present seal until the current commission expires. The secretary of state will issue the notary's next commission for the new county, and the notary should obtain a new seal or stamp then.

Fees

A notary may charge $2.00 per signature for taking and certifying the acknowledgment of the execution of any instrument or writing, $2.00 per person for administering oaths or affirmations without a verification or proof, and $2.00 per signature for a verification or proof.

Some fee collection, however, is restricted. For example, it is illegal for a notary to charge, either directly or indirectly, greater fees than those set by statute.[13] Whether a notary may charge for mileage traveled in order to notarize an instrument is unclear, but a literal reading of G.S. 138-2 indicates that he or she may not. Certain statutory provisions disallow notarial fees in specific situations: A notary who is "an officer, director, agent, or employee" of a bank may be charged with a misdemeanor if he or she receives a fee, directly or indirectly, "on account of any transaction to which the bank is a party."[14] Any person in the business of lending money in the amount of $1,500 or less and licensed under the North Carolina Consumer Finance Act of 1961 "shall not collect or permit to be collected any notary fee in connection with any loan made."[15] When loan documents are

---

12. N.C. Gen. Stat. § 10A-10.

13. *Id.* § 138-2.

14. *Id.* § 53-86. This restriction does not apply to savings and loan associations. *See* N.C. Gen. Stat. § 54B-156.

15. *Id.* § 53-177.

notarized, notarial fees are borne by the lender so that the legal interest rate will not be exceeded through additional service charges. Violation of the Consumer Finance Act is a misdemeanor and relieves the borrower of the obligation to repay the loan.[16]

Liability

The violations of notarial duties that are criminal offenses have been discussed in Chapter I. Only once has a suit against a North Carolina notary for negligence reached the appellate courts. In Nelson v. Comer, a notary certified the acknowledgment of the execution of a deed by a man who claimed to be the owner of the property transferred by the deed.[17] The notary did not ask the man for proof of identity and thus did not discover that he was an impostor. A couple who relied on the fraudulent deed in a later purchase of the property sued the notary for damages caused by his negligence in taking the acknowledgment. The notary was held not liable. The North Carolina Court of Appeals stated: "A public official, engaged in the performance of governmental duties involving the exercise of judgment and discretion, may not be held personally liable for mere negligence in respect thereto."[18] However, a notary whose "act, or failure to act, was corrupt or malicious or . . . outside of and beyond the scope of his duties" could be held personally liable for resulting harm.[19] Thus, for example, a notary who intentionally falsely certifies an acknowledgment may be held personally liable.

---

16. *Id.* § 53-166(c) and (d).
17. 21 N.C. App. 636, 205 S.E.2d 537 (1974).
18. *Id.* at 638, 205 S.E.2d at 538.
19. *Id.*

IV
Certification

Introduction

North Carolina law requires that many transactions be put in writing and made a matter of public record in order to give notice to anyone who may later do business with one of the parties to the transaction.[1] Many written instruments cannot be registered as public records until an authorized official, such as a notary public, certifies that the documents were executed properly.[2] Normally, a person executes a document by signing his name to it. However, if he cannot write his name, North Carolina law recognizes his mark as a valid signature, and a mark may be either acknowledged or proved in the same manner as a signature.[3] Also, if he is physically unable to write, he may have his name signed for him, with his consent and in his presence, by another person.[4] And anyone who is blind or otherwise visually handicapped within the meaning of G.S. 111-11 may use a signature facsimile, which must be registered in the office of the clerk of superior court in the county of the person's residence.[5]

The execution of a document may be certified in either of two ways.[6] In the usual way, the person signing the instrument appears before the notary and either signs it in the notary's presence or identifies an earlier signature as his or her own. This personal appearance is called acknowledgment; that term is also used to describe the notary's written certificate that the acknowledgment occurred.[7]

---

1. *See, e.g.*, N.C. GEN. STAT. §§ 47-18, -20.
2. *Id.* § 47-17.
3. Devereux v. McMahon, 108 N.C. 134, 12 S.E. 902 (1891).
4. Lee v. Parker, 171 N.C. 144, 88 S.E. 217 (1916).
5. N.C. GEN. STAT. § 22A-1.
6. *See id.* § 47-17.
7. 1 AM. JUR. 2D *Acknowledgments* § 1 (1962).

In the second method of certification, a person other than the signer of the instrument appears before the notary and states under oath that (1) the one who signed the instrument signed it in the person's presence, or (2) the signer acknowledged to the person that he or she had signed the instrument, or (3) the person recognizes the signature of either the signer or a subscribing witness as genuine.[8] This procedure is called taking the proof of an instrument. These two means of certifying a written instrument—acknowledgment and proof—and the forms for each are explained in this chapter.

Acknowledgment

Procedure

To acknowledge a written instrument, a person must do the following:

(1) Physically appear before the notary. The acknowledger's actual physical presence before the notary is essential to the validity of the acknowledgment.[9] An attempted acknowledgment by telephone, telegraph, mail, or any other means that does not bring the acknowledger physically before the notary is invalid.[10] And note that it is unethical for an attorney to file a document for public record when the attorney has personal knowledge that the acknowledger did not physically appear before the certifying notary.[11]

(2) Be personally known to the notary or have his or her identity proven on the basis of satisfactory evidence. A notary has "personal knowledge of the identity" of a signer when he or she has been acquainted with the signer for a sufficient time to eliminate every reasonable doubt as to the identity claimed.[12] A notary may establish a signer's identity by "satisfactory evidence of identity" in one of two ways: (1) either the signer furnishes the notary with a current document issued by an agency of the federal or state government with the signer's photograph (for example, a driver's license), *or* (2) the signer is identified by a

---

8. N.C. GEN. STAT. §§ 47-12, -12.1, -13.

9. *Id.* § 10A-3(i).

10. *See* Southern State Bank v. Sumner, 187 N.C. 762, 122 S.E. 848 (1924).

11. N.C. STATE BAR, ETHICAL OPINIONS 720 (1970) (hereinafter cited as ETHICAL OPINION).

12. N.C. GEN. STAT. § 10A-3(7).

credible person who is personally known to the notary and who has personal knowledge of the signer's identity.[13]

(3) Sign the instrument in the presence of the notary, or state to the notary that he or she voluntarily signed the instrument. Generally, the acknowledger signs the document in the presence of the notary; if a writing presented to a notary has already been signed, the notary must obtain an affirmative statement from the acknowledger that the signature is his or hers and that he or she voluntarily signed the instrument.

Failure to meet all of the conditions described in this section may invalidate the acknowledgment and may also subject the notary to revocation of his or her commission.

Acknowledgeable instruments

Any instrument or document may be acknowledged. Many instruments—including deeds, contracts, and leases—must be acknowledged or proved before they may be registered.[14] Among the types of instruments listed in G.S. 47-1 that may be acknowledged are deeds, deeds of trust, leases, powers of attorney, assignments, releases, and affidavits concerning land titles or family history.

Acknowledger

The person signing an instrument is the proper person to acknowledge its execution. Also, an instrument signed by a certain person may be acknowledged by that person's attorney in fact under a power of attorney if the power of attorney so provides.[15] An attorney in fact who signs an instrument for another person under a power of attorney is the proper acknowledger of the instrument.[16]

Order of acknowledgment

When an instrument has been signed by more than one person, the acknowledgments need not be made in the same order as the signatures, nor must the certificates of acknowledgment appear in any particular order. Furthermore, an instrument executed by several different persons may be acknowledged by each of them before the same

---

13. *Id.* § 10A-3(8).

14. *Id.* § 47-17.

15. Cochran v. Linville Improvement Co., 127 N.C. 386, 37 S.E. 496 (1900).

16. *See* N.C. GEN. STAT. §§ 47-43 and -43.1.

notary or before different notaries at different times and in different places.

Federal law

Under federal law, a North Carolina notary may take acknowledgments of deeds and other instruments affecting property located in the District of Columbia.[17] Applications for patents, assignments of patents,[18] trademarks,[19] and claims against the United States[20] may be acknowledged before a notary of this state. A notary may also take acknowledgments of agreements to arbitrate railroad labor disputes[21] and of organization certificates of national banks.[22]

Proof of Execution

Procedure

To prove the execution of a written instrument, a person must

(1) physically appear before the notary,
(2) be personally known to the notary or prove his or her identity on the basis of satisfactory evidence, and
(3) give his or her testimony under oath.

The notary must adhere to provisions (1) and (2) as stringently for a proof of execution as for an acknowledgment (see previous section). For provision (3), although a notary must administer an oath whenever the execution of a document is proved, the statutes provide no specific oath. The following oath suffices:

Do you swear [or affirm] that the information you give concerning this writing is the truth, so help you, God?

The procedure for administering oaths as explained in Chapter V should be followed.

Notaries often do not administer oaths in situations that require them. Although the notary's certificate that the witness was duly sworn is presumptive evidence that the oath was given, questions concerning the

---

17. D.C. Code § 45-403.
18. 35 U.S.C. § 261.
19. *Id.* § 1061.
20. *Id.* § 203.
21. *Id.* § 158(d).
22. *Id.* § 23.

validity of the certificate may be raised if the oath was omitted. Also, a certificate of proof that does not indicate that the person proving the instrument was placed under oath has no legal validity.[23]

Provable instruments

Ordinarily, the signing of any instrument that may be acknowledged may also be proved. The dissent to the will of a deceased spouse must, however, be personally acknowledged by the spouse or his or her attorney. If the spouse is a minor or an incompetent, the dissent may be signed and acknowledged by his or her guardian or, if the spouse has no guardian, by the "next friend" appointed by the clerk of the superior court of the county where the will is probated.[24] Also, the Division of Motor Vehicles (DMV) requires that signatures on title documents be acknowledged rather than proved; if, therefore, a notary uses a proof of execution on a DMV document, the certification will be invalid.

Proof taker

A notary public may take the proof of the signing of any writing that may be proved.[25]

Proof giver

1. Subscribing witnesses. The signing of an instrument may be proved by the sworn testimony of a subscribing witness to the instrument.[26] A subscribing witness is a witness who signed the document. The witness states under oath that the person who executed the instrument either signed it in the witness's presence or acknowledged its execution to him or her.[27] If, however, the subscribing witness is a grantee or beneficiary in the instrument, he or she may not prove the execution of the instrument, nor may his or her signature be proved by anyone else.[28]

2. Other persons. If all of the subscribing witnesses have died, have left the state, or have become incompetent or unavailable, the instrument may be proved by any person who will state under oath that he or she knows the handwriting of the maker of the instrument and that the signature on the instrument is the maker's.[29] The instrument may also be proved

---

23. McClure v. Crow, 196 N.C. 657, 146 S.E. 713 (1929).

24. N.C. GEN. STAT. § 30-2.

25. *Id.* § 47-1.

26. *Id.* § 47-12.

27. *Id.*

28. *Id.* § 47-12.2.

29. N.C. GEN. STAT. § 47-12.1.

if the person states under oath that he or she knows the handwriting of a subscribing witness and that the signature on the document is that of the subscribing witness.[30] Again, if the subscribing witness is a beneficiary or grantee in the instrument, his or her signature may not be proved.

If the instrument has no subscribing witnesses, it may be proved by any person who will state under oath that he or she knows the handwriting of the maker and that the signature on the instrument is the maker's.[31]

Certificate Forms of Acknowledgment and Proof

Introduction

All statutory forms for the certification of acknowledgment or proof of written instruments include

(1) the name of the state and county in which the certification occurs;

(2) the body of the certificate, stating before whom, by whom, and in what manner the signature was acknowledged or proved;

(3) the date of acknowledgment or proof; and

(4) the signature and seal of the officer who took the acknowledgment or proof.[32]

The name of the person whose signature is being acknowledged or proved should be typed or printed in the certificate exactly as it was signed on the document. Some notaries add to their certificates the words "Let the instrument with this certificate be registered" or a similar expression, but this phrase is not required and has no legal significance. The notary's certificate must be written on the document or attached to it in a manner (by glue or staples, for example) making detachment unlikely. When motor vehicle title documents are acknowledged, the acknowledgment must be on the document itself.

Many instruments drafted by the parties or their attorneys have blank certificate forms already attached. Determining whether the certificate has the desired legal effect is the responsibility of the parties and

---

30. *Id.*

31. *Id.* § 47-13.

32. *See, e.g., id.* §§ 47-38 and -41.

their attorneys; the notary's duty is to ensure that the recitals of the certificate are accurate. Many printed instruments include several blank certificates from which the one suitable to the situation must be selected.

When an instrument is presented without a certificate form, or without one that may be adapted to the circumstances, an applicable form should be made out by either a party to the instrument or an attorney and attached to the instrument. Should questions arise about a certificate's validity or suitability, it is usually better to type a new certificate than to alter materially the face of a printed form.

Various forms for certifying the acknowledgment or proof of the execution of instruments are below. An explanation of each form is given, and the blank form, with instructions for completing it, is set out. Then an example of a completed form is shown. The language of most of the forms is statutory; however, some forms derive from statutory requirements providing no precise wording. When the precise language is required by statute, that statute is cited in a footnote.

Although *substantial* compliance with most of the forms is sufficient for legal validity, the statutory wording should be followed closely, because what may seem an inconsequential variation to the notary can actually be an omission or alteration invalidating the certificate. As will be explained later, two of the forms (for maps and plats and for the short-form power of attorney) must contain the exact wording in the statutes or the register of deeds will not record the instrument. The personal pronouns used in the forms, most of which are masculine and singular, should be altered to fit the individual case.   ▼

Instruments executed by individuals

▼   Acknowledgment of instrument signed by one person

When an instrument is executed by a person in his or her individual capacity who personally appears before the notary to acknowledge his or her signature, this is the proper certificate.[33]

North Carolina
_____(A)_____ County

I, _____(B)_____, a Notary Public for said
County and State, do hereby certify that
_____(C)_____ personally appeared before me this
day and acknowledged the due execution of the foregoing instrument.

Witness my hand and official seal, this the ____(D)____
day of ____(E)____, 19 _(F)_.

(Official Seal)   _____(G)_____
                                                Notary Public

My commission expires _____(H)_____, 19 _(I)_.

A. Name of county where acknowledgment is taken.

B. Typed or printed name of notary exactly as it appears on the seal or stamp.

C. Typed or printed name of person whose acknowledgment is being taken exactly as it appears on the signature line.

D. Date acknowledgment taken.

E. Month acknowledgment taken.

F. Year acknowledgment taken.

G. Signature of notary.

H. Date and month notary's commission expires.

I. Year notary's commission expires.

---

33. *Id.* § 47-38.

Example: Slim Beane appears before John Apple, an Alexander County notary, to execute a deed on March 15, 1991. Apple's commission expires April 15, 1995. The acknowledgment is taken in Taylorsville.

```
North Carolina
      Alexander          County

I, _____John Apple_____, a Notary Public for said
County and State, do hereby certify that
_____Slim Beane_____ personally appeared before me this
day and acknowledged the due execution of the forego-
ing instrument.

Witness my hand and official seal, this the ___15th___
day of ___March___, 19 _91_.

(Official Seal)                    John Apple
                                 Notary Public

My commission expires _____April 15_____, 19 _95_.
```

▼ Acknowledgment of instrument signed by two or more persons

When an instrument is executed by two or more persons and their acknowledgments are taken before different notaries at different times, each notary must execute a certificate for the individual whose acknowledgment is being taken, as indicated previously. If their acknowledgments are taken before the same notary at the same time, the proper form is above.[34]

North Carolina
_____(A)_____ County

I, _____(B)_____, a Notary Public for said County and State, do hereby certify that _____(C)_____ and _____(D)_____ personally appeared before me this day and acknowledged the due execution of the foregoing instrument.

Witness my hand and official seal, this the ___(E)___ day of ___(F)___, 19 _(G)_.

(Official Seal)   _____(H)_____
                                              Notary Public

My commission expires _____(I)_____, 19 _(J)_.

A. Name of county where acknowledgment is taken.

B. Typed or printed name of notary exactly as it appears on the seal or stamp.

C. Typed or printed name of first person whose acknowledgment is being taken exactly as it appears on the signature line.

D. Typed or printed name of second person whose acknowledgment is being taken exactly as it appears on the signature line.

E. Date acknowledgment taken.

F. Month acknowledgment taken.

G. Year acknowledgment taken.

H. Signature of notary.

I. Date and month notary's commission expires.

J. Year notary's commission expires.

---

34. *See* N.C. Gen. Stat. § 47-40.

Example: Ruby Jewell and Opal Jewell appear before Melville Hawthorne, an Anson County notary, to execute a deed on July 6, 1991. Hawthorne's commission expires December 1, 1993. The acknowledgments are taken in Wadesboro.

North Carolina
_____Anson_____ County

I, _Melville Hawthorne_, a Notary Public for said County and State, do hereby certify that _Ruby Jewell_ and _Opal Jewell_ personally appeared before me this day and acknowledged the due execution of the foregoing instrument.

Witness my hand and official seal, this the _6th_ day of _July_, 19 _91_.

(Official Seal)   *Melville Hawthorne*
                                        Notary Public

My commission expires _December 1_, 19 _93_.

▼   Acknowledgment by attorney in fact

The statutes require that an acknowledgment by an attorney in fact under a power of attorney be given under oath. Since no oath is specified, the oath found on page 20 will satisfy the requirement. When an instrument is executed for another person by an attorney in fact under a power of attorney, the acknowledgment should be certified as follows:[35]

---

35. *Id.* § 47-43.

North Carolina
_____(A)_____ County

I, _____(B)_____, a Notary Public for said County and
State, do hereby certify that _____(C)_____, attorney
in fact for _____(D)_____, personally appeared before
me this day, and being by me duly sworn, says that he
executed the foregoing and annexed instrument for and in
behalf of the said _____(E)_____, and that his authority to execute and acknowledge said instrument is
contained in an instrument duly executed, acknowledged,
and recorded in the office of _____(F)_____ in the
County of _____(G)_____, State of _____(H)_____,
on the ____(I)____ day of ____(J)____, 19_(K)_, and that this
instrument was executed under and by virtue of the
authority given by said instrument granting him power of
attorney.
        I do further certify that the said _____(L)_____
acknowledged the due execution of the foregoing and annexed instrument for the purposes therein expressed for
and in behalf of the said _____(M)_____.

Witness my hand and official seal, this the ____(N)____ day
of ____(O)____, 19 _(P)_.

(Official Seal)   _____(Q)_____
                                          Notary Public

My commission expires _____(R)_____, 19 _(S)_.

A. Name of county where acknowledgment is taken.
B. Typed or printed name of notary exactly as it appears in the seal or stamp.
C. Typed or printed name of attorney in fact exactly as it appears on the signature line.
D. Typed or printed name of principal (person giving the power of attorney) exactly as it appears on the signature line.
E. Typed or printed name of principal exactly as it appears on the signature line.
F. Name of office where power of attorney is recorded.
G. Name of county where power of attorney is recorded.
H. Name of state where power of attorney is recorded.
I. Date power of attorney was recorded.
J. Month power of attorney was recorded.
K. Year power of attorney was recorded.
L. Typed or printed name of attorney in fact exactly as it appears on the signature line.
M. Typed or printed name of principal exactly as it appears on the signature line.
N. Date acknowledgment taken.
O. Month acknowledgment taken.
P. Year acknowledgment taken.
Q. Signature of notary.
R. Date and month notary's commission expires.
S. Year notary's commission expires.

Example: May Ishmael gave her power of attorney to George Ishmael, and the instrument was recorded in the Dare County registry on June 30, 1989. On August 14, 1991, George executes a deed on behalf of May and acknowledges the execution before Sherlock Watson, a Hyde County notary. Watson's commission expires November 26, 1992. The acknowledgment is taken in Swan Quarter.

North Carolina
_____ Hyde _____ County

I, _____ Sherlock Watson ___, a Notary Public for said County and State, do hereby certify that _____ George Ishmael ___, attorney in fact for ___ May Ishmael _____, personally appeared before me this day, and being by me duly sworn, says that he executed the foregoing and annexed instrument for and in behalf of the said _____ May Ishmael ___, and that his authority to execute and acknowledge said instrument is contained in an instrument duly executed, acknowledged, and recorded in the office of the register of deeds in the County of _____ Dare _____, State of ___ North Carolina ___, on the ___ 30th ___ day of _____ June ___, 19 89, and that this instrument was executed under and by virtue of the authority given by said instrument granting him power of attorney.

I do further certify that the said ___ George Ishmael ___ acknowledged the due execution of the foregoing and annexed instrument for the purposes therein expressed for and in behalf of the said _____ May Ishmael _____.

Witness my hand and official seal, this the ___ 14th ___ day of ___ August ___, 19 __91__.

(Official Seal)   *Sherlock Watson*
                                    _____
                                         Notary Public

My commission expires _____ November 26 _____, 19 __92__.

▼   Proof by subscribing witness

As described earlier, an instrument that has one or more subscribing witnesses may be proved by the sworn testimony of one of these witnesses. The form of the certificate is shown here.[36]

```
North Carolina
        (A)
_____ County


I, _____(B)_____ , a notary public of
_____(C)_____ County, _____(D)_____ , cer-
tify that _____(E)_____ personally appeared
before me this day, and being duly sworn, stated
that in his presence _____(F)_____ (signed) (ac-
knowledged the execution of) the foregoing instrument.


Witness my hand and official seal, this the ___(G)____
day of ____(H)____ , 19 _(I)_.


(Official Seal)                        _____(J)_____
                                        Notary  Public


My commission expires _____(K)_____ , 19 _(L)_ .
```

A. Name of county where proof is taken.
B. Typed or printed name of notary exactly as it appears in the seal or stamp.
C. Name of county where notary is commissioned.
D. Name of state where notary is commissioned.
E. Typed or printed name of witness proving the document exactly as this name appears from his or her signature as a subscribing witness to the instrument.
F. Typed or printed name of person who executed the instrument being proved exactly as this name appears on the signature line.
G. Date proof taken.
H. Month proof taken.
I. Year proof taken.
J. Signature of notary.
K. Date and month notary's commission expires.
L. Year notary's commission expires.

---

36. *Id.* § 47-43.2.

Example: Narley Pratt executes a deed to his land in Madison County. Shepard Ladd is a subscribing witness to Pratt's execution of the deed. On November 11, 1991, Ladd appears before Bonnie Doone, a Buncombe County notary, to prove the execution of the instrument. Doone's commission expires July 1, 1995. The proof is taken in Asheville.

North Carolina
          Buncombe   County

I,   Bonnie Doone   , a notary public of
        Buncombe   County,   North Carolina   , cer-
tify that   Shepard Ladd   personally appeared
before me this day, and being duly sworn, stated
that in his presence   Narley Pratt   signed (~~ac-~~
~~knowledged the execution of~~) the foregoing instrument.

Witness my hand and official seal, this the   11th
day of   November   , 19   91 .

(Official Seal)   *Bonnie Doone*
                                        Notary Public

My commission expires   July 1   , 19   95 .

▼ Proof by other person: signature of person who executed

When there are no subscribing witnesses to an instrument or they are unavailable, the execution of the instrument may be proved by a person who can recognize the handwriting of either the person who executed the instrument[37] or a subscribing witness.[38] The proper forms for these methods of proof are here and on pages 34–35:

North Carolina

_____(A)_____ County

I, _____(B)_____, a notary public of
_____(C)_____ County, _____(D)_____, certify
that _____(E)_____ personally appeared before me
this day, and being duly sworn, stated that he knows
the handwriting of _____(F)_____ and that the
signature to the foregoing instrument is the signature of _____(G)_____ .

Witness my hand and official seal, this the ___(H)___
day of ___(I)___, 19 _(J)_.

(Official Seal)   _____(K)_____
                       Notary Public

My commission expires _____(L)_____, 19 _(M)_.

A. Name of county where proof is taken.
B. Typed or printed name of notary exactly as it appears in the seal or stamp.
C. Name of county where notary is commissioned.
D. Name of state where notary is commissioned.
E. Typed or printed name of person proving the signature.
F. Typed or printed name of person who executed the instrument being proved exactly as this name appears on the signature line.

G. Typed or printed name of person who executed the instrument being proved exactly as this name appears on the signature line.
H. Date proof taken.
I. Month proof taken.
J. Year proof taken.
K. Signature of notary.
L. Date and month notary's commission expires.
M. Year notary's commission expires.

---

37. *Id.* § 47-43.3.
38. *Id.* § 47-43.4.

Example: Knox Calvin executes a deed to his property in Franklin County. On February 3, 1991, Francis Xavier appears before Stormy Skye, a Franklin County notary, to prove Calvin's signature on the instrument. Skye's commission expires October 13, 1993. The proof is taken in Louisburg.

North Carolina
_____Franklin_____ County

I, _____Stormy Skye_____, a notary public of
_____Franklin_____ County, ____North Carolina____, certify
that _____Francis Xavier_____ personally appeared before me
this day, and being duly sworn, stated that he knows
the handwriting of _____Knox Calvin_____ and that the
signature to the foregoing instrument is the signature of _____Knox Calvin_____.

Witness my hand and official seal, this the ____3rd____
day of __February__, 19 _91_.

(Official Seal)   _____Stormy Skye_____
                              Notary Public

My commission expires _____October 13_____, 19 _93_.

▼ Proof by other person: signature of subscribing witness

North Carolina
_____(A)_____ County

I, _____(B)_____, a notary public of
_____(C)_____ County, _____(D)_____, certify
that _____(E)_____ personally appeared before me
this day, and being duly sworn, stated that he knows
the handwriting of _____(F)_____, and that the
signature of _____(G)_____ as a subscribing
witness to the foregoing instrument is the signature
of _____(H)_____.

Witness my hand and official seal, this the ___(I)___
day of ___(J)___, 19 _(K)_.

(Official Seal)   _____(L)_____
                                          Notary Public

My commission expires _____(M)_____, 19 _(N)_.

A. Name of county where proof is taken.

B. Typed or printed name of notary exactly as it appears in the seal or stamp.

C. Name of county where notary is commissioned.

D. Name of state where notary is commissioned.

E. Typed or printed name of person proving the signature of the subscribing witness.

F. Typed or printed name of subscribing witness exactly as it appears on the signature line.

G. Typed or printed name of subscribing witness exactly as it appears on the signature line.

H. Typed or printed name of subscribing witness exactly as it appears on the signature line.

I. Date proof taken.

J. Month proof taken.

K. Year proof taken.

L. Signature of notary.

M. Date and month notary's commission expires.

N. Year notary's commission expires.

Example: John Little executes a deed to his land in Columbus County, with Ernest Mann as a subscribing witness. On March 30, 1991, Earl Grey appears before Ashley Lee Cavanaugh, a Columbus County notary, to prove Mann's signature as a subscribing witness. Cavanaugh's commission expires March 31, 1995. The proof is taken in Whiteville.

North Carolina

_____Columbus_____ County

I, _Ashley Lee Cavanaugh_, a notary public of _____Columbus_____ County, ___North Carolina___, certify that _____Earl Grey_____ personally appeared before me this day, and being duly sworn, stated that he knows the handwriting of _____Ernest Mann_____, and that the signature of _____Ernest Mann_____ as a subscribing witness to the foregoing instrument is the signature of _____Ernest Mann_____.

Witness my hand and official seal, this the ___30th___ day of ___March___, 19 _91_.

(Official Seal)   *Ashley Lee Cavanaugh*
                                  Notary Public

My commission expires ____March 31____, 19 _95_.

Instruments executed by trustees

A trust is an arrangement in which property, either real or personal, is managed by a trustee for the benefit of another person, the beneficiary. Instruments executed by a person as trustee are his or her own acts and must be acknowledged or proved in the manner set forth in the preceding sections for individuals. A trustee should sign an instrument in a manner that indicates the capacity in which he or she acts, and the certificate of acknowledgment or proof should indicate that he or she has signed as trustee.[39]

▼   **Example of execution by trustee:**

> *Joe Colorado*
> _____
> Joe Colorado
> Trustee for Roger Hill

The text of the acknowledgment should read:

> I, _____, a Notary Public
> for said County and State, do hereby
> certify that Joe Colorado, Trustee for
> Roger Hill, personally appeared before
> me this day and acknowledged the due
> execution of the foregoing instrument.

---

39. *See* Hayes v. Ferguson, 206 N.C. 414, 174 S.E. 121 (1934).

Instruments executed by partnerships

A partnership is an unincorporated association of two or more persons formed to do business for profit.[40] Within certain limits, the business-related acts of a partner will bind the other partners.[41] Real property belonging to a partnership must be conveyed in the name of the partnership, but ordinarily any one of the partners may execute the conveyance in the partnership name.[42] The forms for acknowledgment or proof of instruments executed by individuals may be used for certificates of individual partners, and the certificates should indicate the capacity in which the individual partners sign.

▼ Example of execution by partner:

John R. Tweedledum

T & T Hats, A Partnership,
by John R. Tweedledum, a partner

The text of the acknowledgment should read:

I, _____, a Notary Public for said County and State, do hereby certify that John R. Tweedledum, a partner in T & T Hats, personally appeared before me this day and acknowledged the due execution of the foregoing instrument.

---

40. N.C. Gen. Stat. § 59-36.
41. *Id.* § 59-39.
42. *Id.* §§ 59-38(c) and -39.

Instruments executed by persons doing business under assumed names

Persons doing business under assumed names—other than partnership or corporation names—should sign documents concerning their business in a manner indicating the capacity in which they act, and the certificate of acknowledgment or proof should indicate this capacity.

▼   **Example of execution under an assumed name:**

Zoot Hawkins/Doing business as (DBA)
Hot Shot Records

The text of the acknowledgment should read as follows:

I, _____, a Notary Public
for said County and State, do hereby
certify that _Zoot Hawkins/DBA Hot Shot_
_Records_____ personally appeared before
me this day and acknowledged the due
execution of the foregoing instrument.

Instruments executed by religious bodies or denominations

The trustees of any religious body may mortgage or sell land owned by the religious group when the group directs them to do so.[43] The trustees should sign the instrument in a manner indicating the capacity in which they act, and the certificate of acknowledgment or proof should indicate this capacity. The form of the certificate is the one used for individuals.

▼   **Example of execution by church trustees:**

> *John MacDuff, Hugh MacBeth, Hamish Malcolm*
> John MacDuff, Hugh MacBeth, Hamish Malcolm
> Trustees for Church of the Rock

The text of the acknowledgment should read as follows:

> I, _____, Notary Public
> for said County and State, do hereby
> certify that John MacDuff, Hugh MacBeth,
> Hamish Malcolm, Trustees for Church of the Rock,
> personally appeared before me this day
> and acknowledged the due execution of
> the foregoing instrument.

In addition, ecclesiastical officers, such as ministers or bishops, designated by a religious group to administer its affairs may convey the property of that group.[44] The execution by such an officer is acknowledged or proved in the same manner as an execution by an individual, and the certificate of acknowledgment should indicate the capacity in which the ecclesiastical officer signed.

---

43. *Id.* § 61-4.
44. *Id.* § 61-5.

▼ **Example of execution by an ecclesiastical officer:**

Joseph Victor McCarroll
Joseph Victor McCarroll,
Bishop of the Carolinas

The text of the acknowledgment should read as follows:

I, _____, a Notary Public
for said County and State, do hereby
certify that   Joseph Victor McCarroll,
Bishop of the Carolinas,   personally
appeared before me this day and
acknowledged the due execution of
the foregoing instrument.

Instruments executed by voluntary associations

A voluntary association of persons organized for charitable, fraternal, religious, social, or patriotic purposes may hold real property either through trustees or in the association's name.[45] Property held through trustees may be conveyed by an instrument executed by them as trustees and acknowledged or proved in the manner previously described for individuals.[46] The notary adds to his or her certificate the fact that they have executed the instrument as trustees of the named association. When the transaction is authorized by the voluntary association, real estate held in the association's name may be conveyed "by a deed signed by its chairman or president, and its secretary or treasurer, or such officer as is the custodian of its common seal with its official seal affixed, the said conveyance to be proven and probated in the same manner as provided by law for deeds by corporations . . . ."[47]

Forms for proving the execution of corporate conveyances are set out below. In applying the forms to conveyances by voluntary associations,

---

45. N.C. Gen. Stat. §§ 39-24 and -26.
46. *Id.* § 39-26.
47. *Id.* § 39-25.

the phrase *voluntary association* should be substituted wherever the word *corporation* appears, and the term *common seal* should replace *corporate seal.*

Instruments executed by corporations

The law carefully specifies the methods by which corporate authority may be delegated, exercised, and authenticated,[48] because a corporation is a legal person separate from the individuals who are its officers, directors, and stockholders; it is bound only by the authorized acts of its agents. Adherence to the statutory requirements and forms ensures that corporate instruments are legitimate acts of the corporation rather than unauthorized acts of individuals.

Instruments executed by corporations will usually include the necessary certificate forms. Whenever a notary prepares his or her own certificate of acknowledgment or proof for an instrument executed by a corporation, he or she should select the form in this section that fits the particular circumstances.

G.S. 47-41.01 and -41.02 set out four different forms of acknowledgment that may be used for a corporate deed, deed of trust, or other instrument conveying an interest in real estate. The form in G.S. 47-41.01 and the third form in G.S. 47-41.02 both certify an instrument that has three essential components: (1) the instrument is executed by one officer of the corporation, (2) the instrument is attested (witnessed) by another officer of the corporation, and (3) the corporate seal is affixed.

---

48. *See, e.g., id.* §§ 55-8-40, 55-8-41, 47-41.01.

▼ Instruments conveying security interest in personal property of a corporation

When a contract creates a security interest in the personal property of a corporation, the contract will usually be signed by one of the following corporate officers: the president, a vice-president, the secretary, an assistant secretary, the treasurer, or an assistant treasurer. The statutes do not require that such contracts bear the corporate seal or be attested by another corporate officer.[49] Here is the proper acknowledgment form for these contracts:

North Carolina

_____(A)_____ County

I, _____(B)_____, a Notary Public for said County and State, do hereby certify that _____(C)_____ personally came before me this day and acknowledged that he is _____(D)_____ of _____(E)_____ and acknowledged, on behalf of _____(F)_____, the due execution of the foregoing instrument.

Witness my hand and official seal, this the ___(G)___ day of ___(H)___, 19 _(I)_.

(Official Seal)   _____(J)_____

                             Notary Public

My commission expires _____(K)_____, 19 _(L)_.

A. Name of county where acknowledgment is taken.

B. Typed or printed name of notary exactly as it appears in the seal or stamp.

C. Typed or printed name of corporate officer executing the document exactly as this name appears on the signature line.

D. Title of corporate officer executing the instrument.

E. Name of corporation of which the person who signs is an officer.

F. Name of corporation of which the person who signs is an officer.

G. Date acknowledgment taken.

H. Month acknowledgment taken.

I. Year acknowledgment taken.

J. Signature of notary.

K. Date and month notary's commission expires.

L. Year notary's commission expires.

---

49. *See id.* § 47-41.02(f).

Example: Timothy Cruise, president of the Juice & Sauce Corporation, executes a document giving a security interest in the corporation's personal property to First National Bank. Cruise appears before Tuesday Morning, a Duplin County notary, on July 3, 1991, to acknowledge execution of the instrument. Morning's commission expires July 4, 1991. The acknowledgment is taken in Kenansville.

North Carolina
_____Duplin_____ County

I, ___Tuesday Morning___, a Notary Public for said County and State, do hereby certify that ___Timothy Cruise___ personally came before me this day and acknowledged that he is _____President_____ of Juice & Sauce Corporation and acknowledged, on behalf of Juice & Sauce Corporation, the due execution of the foregoing instrument.

Witness my hand and official seal, this the ___3rd___ day of ___July___, 19 _91_.

(Official Seal)   *Tuesday Morning*
                                   Notary Public

My commission expires _____July 4_____, 19 _91_.

▼ Acknowledgment by attesting officer

For this form to be used, the instrument must have been executed by the chairman, chief executive officer, president, vice-president, assistant vice-president, treasurer, or chief financial officer. It must have been attested by the secretary, assistant secretary, trust officer, assistant trust officer, associate trust officer, or—in the case of a bank—the secretary, assistant secretary, cashier, or assistant cashier.[50] The officer signing the instrument must do so in the name of the corporation. Only the attesting officer need appear before the notary to give the acknowledgment.

```
North Carolina
_____(A)_____ County


I, _____(B)_____, Notary Public for said County
and State, certify that _____(C)_____ personally
came before me this day and acknowledged that he is
_____(D)_____ of _____(E)_____, a corpora-
tion, and that by authority duly given and as the
act of the corporation the foregoing instrument was
signed in its name by its _____(F)_____, sealed
with its corporate seal, and attested by himself as
its _____(G)_____.


Witness my hand and official seal, this the ___(H)___
day of ___(I)___, 19 (J).


(Official Seal)                    _____(K)_____
                                     Notary Public


My commission expires _____(L)_____, 19 (M).
```

A. Name of county where acknowledgment taken.

B. Typed or printed name of notary exactly as it appears in the seal or stamp.

C. Typed or printed name of officer attesting the instrument's execution exactly as this name appears on the signature line of the attestation.

D. Title of officer attesting.

E. Name of corporation.

F. Title of officer signing the instrument.

G. Title of attesting officer.

H. Date acknowledgment taken.

I. Month acknowledgment taken.

J. Year acknowledgment taken.

K. Notary's signature.

L. Date and month notary's commission expires.

M. Year notary's commission expires.

---

50. N.C. Gen. Stat. § 47-41.01.

Example: Jenny Longfellow, president of Walden Grits Company, executes a deed to corporate property, and Melissa Thoreau, secretary of the company, attests the execution. On August 11, 1991, Thoreau appears before Henry Wadsworth, a Guilford County notary, to acknowledge the instrument. Wadsworth's commission expires September 15, 1995. The acknowledgment is taken in Greensboro.

North Carolina
_____Guilford_____ County

I, _____Henry Wadsworth_____, Notary Public for said County
and State, certify that _____Melissa Thoreau_____ personally
came before me this day and acknowledged that she is
_____Secretary_____ of _____Walden Grits Company_____, a corporation, and that by authority duly given and as the
act of the corporation the foregoing instrument was
signed in its name by its _____President_____, sealed
with its corporate seal, and attested by herself as
its _____Secretary_____.

Witness my hand and official seal, this the _____11th_____
day of _____August_____, 19 _91_.

(Official Seal)

Henry W Wadsworth
Notary Public

My commission expires _____September 15_____, 19 _95_.

▼   Acknowledgment by signing officer

The form set out below is for use when the corporate officer who executed the instrument acknowledges its execution. For this form to be used, the instrument must have been executed by the president, vice-president, presiding member, or trustee of the corporation and attested by its secretary or assistant secretary.[51] The officer acknowledging its execution must be placed under oath.

North Carolina
_____(A)_____ County

This _____(B)_____ day of _____(C)_____, 19_(D)_, personally came before me, _____(E)_____, Notary Public for said County and State, _____(F)_____, who, being by me duly sworn, says that he is _____(G)_____ of the _____(H)_____, a corporation, and that the seal affixed to the foregoing instrument in writing is the corporate seal of said company, and that said writing was signed and sealed by him in behalf of said corporation by its authority duly given. And the said _____(I)_____ acknowledged the said writing to be the act and deed of said corporation.

Witness my hand and official seal, this the _____(J)_____ day of _____(K)_____, 19 _(L)_.

(Official Seal)   _____(M)_____
                              Notary Public

My commission expires _____(N)_____, 19 _(O)_.

A. Name of county where acknowledgment taken.

B. Date acknowledgment taken.

C. Month acknowledgment taken.

D. Year acknowledgment taken.

E. Typed or printed name of notary exactly as it appears in the seal or stamp.

F. Typed or printed name of officer who executed the instrument exactly as it appears on the signature line.

G. Title of officer who executed the instrument.

H. Name of corporation.

I. Typed or printed name of officer who executed the instrument exactly as it appears on the signature line.

J. Date acknowledgment taken.

K. Month acknowledgment taken.

L. Year acknowledgment taken.

M. Notary's signature.

N. Date and month notary's commission expires.

O. Year notary's commission expires.

---

51. *Id.* § 47-41.02.

Example: Sara Lee Baker, president of New River Steel Company, executes a deed to corporate property. Her signature is attested by the corporate secretary, Bonnie Amy Sink. Baker acknowledges execution of the instrument on November 12, 1991, before Homer Scrub, an Ashe County notary. Scrub's commission expires December 13, 1993. The acknowledgment is taken in Jefferson.

North Carolina
_____Ashe_____ County

This ___12th___ day of ___November___, 19_91_, personally came before me, _____Homer Scrub_____, Notary Public for said County and State, ___Sara Lee Baker___, who, being by me duly sworn, says that she is ___President___ of the _New River Steel Company_, a corporation, and that the seal affixed to the foregoing instrument in writing is the corporate seal of said company, and that said writing was signed and sealed by her in behalf of said corporation by its authority duly given. And the said ___Sara Lee Baker___ acknowledged the said writing to be the act and deed of said corporation.

Witness my hand and official seal, this the ___12th___ day of ___November___, 19 _91_.

(Official Seal)   _Homer Scrub_
                                   Notary Public

My commission expires ___December 13___, 19 _93_.

Maps and Plats

Any map or plat presented to the register of deeds for registration must meet specific requirements of size, content, and reproducibility. The land surveyor who prepared the map or plat must execute the certificate set out below.[52]

```
    I, _____, certify that this plat
was drawn under my supervision from an actual
survey made under my supervision (deed description
recorded in Book ___, page ___, etc.) (other);
that the boundaries not surveyed are clearly
indicated as drawn from information found in Book
___, page ___; that the ratio of precision as
calculated is 1:___; that this plat was prepared
in accordance with G.S. 47-30 as amended. Witness
my original signature, registration number and
seal this _____ day of _____, 19___.

Seal or Stamp              _____
                                    Surveyor

                           _____
                           Registration Number
```

The notary must then take the land surveyor's acknowledgment with the following certificate. The exact language of this certificate is required by statute and must be followed word for word.[53] Any deviation will cause the register of deeds to reject the map or plat when it is offered for registration.

---

52. *Id.* § 47-30.
53. *See id.*

```
North Carolina
        (A)            County


I, a Notary Public of the County and State aforesaid,
certify that         (B)         , a registered land
surveyor, personally appeared before me this day and
acknowledged the execution of the foregoing instru-
ment. Witness my hand and official stamp or seal,
this the   (C)    day of     (D)    , 19 (E) .

(Official seal or stamp)                    (F)
                                    _____
                                    Notary Public
                              [_____(G)_____]

My commission expires _____(H)_____, 19 (I) .
```

A. Name of county where acknowledgment taken.

B. Typed or printed name of registered land surveyor exactly as it appears on the signature line of his certificate.

C. Date acknowledgment taken.

D. Month acknowledgment taken.

E. Year acknowledgment taken.

F. Notary's signature.

G. Because no space is in the text of the acknowledgment for the notary's typed or printed name, it is a good idea to add it in brackets just below the signature line. It should appear exactly as in the notary's seal or stamp.

H. Date and month notary's commission expires.

I. Year notary's commission expires.

```
North Carolina
        Orange         County


I, a Notary Public of the County and State aforesaid,
certify that   John I. Mercator  , a registered land sur-
veyor, personally appeared before me this day and ac-
knowledged the execution of the foregoing instrument.
Witness my hand and official stamp or seal, this the
   10th   day of    January , 19 92 .  Patience Noble

(Official seal or stamp)            _____
                                    Notary Public
                              [    Patience Noble    ]

My commission expires        March 5        , 19 95 .
```

Example: John I. Mercator, a registered land surveyor, prepares a plat of a parcel of land in Orange County. On January 10, 1992, he appears before Patience Noble, an Orange County notary, to acknowledge the execution of his certificate on the plat. Noble's commission expires March 5, 1995. The acknowledgment is taken in Carrboro.

Short-Form Powers of Attorney

G.S. 32A-1 sets out a statutory form for a power of attorney, called a "Short Form of General Power of Attorney." Any power of attorney that follows this form will recite in its heading that it is granting powers as defined in Chapter 32A. A power of attorney executed pursuant to this statute must be acknowledged with the certificate below. The exact language of this certificate is required by statute and must be followed word for word.[54] Note that the person acknowledging the execution must be placed under oath. Any deviation from the statutory language of the certificate will cause the register of deeds to reject the power of attorney when it is offered for registration.

```
State of _____(A)_____
County of _____(B)_____

On this ____(C)____ day of ____(D)____, 19 _(E)_,
personally appeared before me, the said named
_____(F)_____, to me known and known to me to be
the person described in and who executed the forego-
ing instrument and he acknowledged that he executed
the same and being duly sworn by me, made oath that
the statements in the foregoing instrument are true.

My commission expires _____(G)_____, 19 _(H)_.

                                  _____
                                         (I)
                                  Notary  Public
                            [_____(J)_____]

                            (Official seal or stamp)
```

A. Name of state where acknowledgment taken.

B. Name of county where acknowledgment taken.

C. Date acknowledgment taken.

D. Month acknowledgment taken.

E. Year acknowledgment taken.

F. Typed or printed name of person executing the power of attorney exactly as this name appears on the signature line.

G. Date and month notary's commission expires.

H. Year notary's commission expires.

I. Notary's signature.

J. Because no space is in the text of the acknowledgment for the notary's typed or printed name, it is a good idea to add it in brackets just below the signature line. It should appear exactly as in the notary's seal or stamp.

---

54. *See id.* § 32A-1.

Example: George Brown executes a short-form power of attorney to his wife, Grace. He appears before Natalie Farrantino, a Tyrrell County notary, on August 14, 1991, to acknowledge execution of the instrument. Farrantino's commission expires September 3, 1991. The acknowledgment is taken in Columbia.

State of ___North Carolina___
County of _____Tyrrell_____

On this ___14th___ day of ___August___, 19 _91_, personally appeared before me, the said named ___George Brown___, to me known and known to me to be the person described in and who executed the forego-ing instrument and he acknowledged that he executed the same and being duly sworn by me, made oath that the statements in the foregoing instrument are true.

My commission expires ___September 3___, 19 _91_.

Natalie Farrantino

Notary Public
[___Natalie Farrantino___]

(Official seal or stamp)

Wills

Ordinary attested wills

An ordinary attested will is attested by two witnesses, and its execution need not be acknowledged or proved before a notary.[55] Such a will is probated by having the witnesses to the will appear before the clerk of superior court and answer certain questions.[56]

Self-proved wills   ▶

Most wills executed today are self-proved; that is, they are executed in accordance with certain statutory requirements, and the witnesses therefore need not appear before the clerk of superior court to prove the will, the proof being contained in the document itself.[57] For a will to be self-proved, a notary or other officer authorized to administer oaths is required. A will can be made self-proving in two ways, the first of which is when it is executed and attested. For this way, the following certificates are used.[58] Note that the testator (person making the will) and the witnesses must be placed under oath.

A. Typed or printed name of person executing will.

B. Date will executed.

C. Month will executed.

D. Year will executed.

E. Signature of person executing will.

F. Typed or printed name of first witness to will.

G. Typed or printed name of second witness to will.

H. Signature of first witness to will.

I. Signature of second witness to will.

J. Name of state where acknowledgment taken.

K. Name of county where acknowledgment taken.

L. Typed or printed name of person executing will.

M. Typed or printed name of first witness to will.

N. Typed or printed name of second witness to will.

O. Date acknowledgment taken. This and the following dates should all agree with the dates of execution of the will.

P. Month acknowledgment taken.

Q. Year acknowledgment taken.

R. Notary's signature.

S. Date and month notary's commission expires.

T. Year notary's commission expires.

---

55. *See* N.C. Gen. Stat. § 31-3.3.
56. *See id.* § 31-18.1.
57. *Id.* § 31-11.6(a).
58. *Id.* § 31-11.6(b).

    I, _____(A)_____, the testator, sign my name to this instrument this __(B)__ day of ____(C)____, 19_(D)_, and being first duly sworn, do hereby declare to the undersigned authority that I sign and execute this instrument as my last will and that I sign it willingly (or willingly direct another to sign for me), that I execute it as my free and voluntary act for the purposes therein expressed, and that I am eighteen years of age or older, of sound mind, and under no constraint or undue influence.

_____(E)_____
                        Testator

    We, _____(F)_____, _____(G)_____, the witnesses, sign our names to this instrument, being first duly sworn, and do hereby declare to the undersigned authority that the testator signs and executes this instrument as his last will and that he signs it willingly (or willingly directs another to sign for him), and that each of us, in the presence and hearing of the testator, hereby signs this will as witness to the testator's signing, and to the best of our knowledge the testator is eighteen years of age or older, of sound mind, and under no constraint or undue influence.

_____(H)_____
                        Witness
_____(I)_____
                        Witness

The State of _____(J)_____
County of _____(K)_____

Subscribed, sworn to and acknowledged before me by _____(L)_____, the testator, and subscribed and sworn to before me by _____(M)_____ and _____(N)_____, witnesses, this __(O)__ day of _____(P)_____, 19_(Q)_.

(Official Seal)   _____(R)_____
                                   Notary Public

My commission expires _____(S)_____, 19_(T)_.

Example: On February 14, 1991, Roberto Cassini executes his will, with ▶
Halston Dior and Polo Dior as witnesses. The acknowledgments to make
the will self-proving are taken before a Forsyth County notary, Jules Tiffany.
Tiffany's commission expires April 15, 1993. The will is executed and acknowledged in Rural Hall.

I, <u>Roberto Cassini</u>, the testator, sign my name to this instrument this <u>14th</u> day of <u>February</u>, 19<u>91</u>, and being first duly sworn, do hereby declare to the undersigned authority that I sign and execute this instrument as my last will and that I sign it willingly (or willingly direct another to sign for me), that I execute it as my free and voluntary act for the purposes therein expressed, and that I am eighteen years of age or older, of sound mind, and under no constraint or undue influence.

<u>*Roberto Cassini*</u>
Testator

We, <u>Halston Dior</u>, <u>Polo Dior</u>, the witnesses, sign our names to this instrument, being first duly sworn, and do hereby declare to the undersigned authority that the testator signs and executes this instrument as his last will and that he signs it willingly (or willingly directs another to sign for him), and that each of us, in the presence and hearing of the testator, hereby signs this will as witness to the testator's signing, and to the best of our knowledge the testator is eighteen years of age or older, of sound mind, and under no constraint or undue influence.

<u>*Halston Dior*</u>
Witness

<u>*Polo Dior*</u>
Witness

The State of <u>North Carolina</u>
County of <u>Forsyth</u>.

Subscribed, sworn to and acknowledged before me by <u>Roberto Cassini</u>, the testator, and subscribed and sworn to before me by <u>Halston Dior</u> and <u>Polo Dior</u>, witnesses, this <u>14th</u> day of <u>February</u>, 19<u>91</u>.

(Official Seal)

<u>*Fuller Tippay*</u>
Notary Public

My commission expires <u>April 15</u>, 19<u>93</u>.

The second way that a will may be made self-proving is for the ▶ testator and witnesses of an already executed and attested will to come before a notary or other officer authorized to administer oaths and make the required acknowledgments using the following certificate.[59] Note that the notary must place the parties under oath.

A. Name of county or city where acknowledgment taken.

B. Typed or printed name of person who executed will.

C. Typed or printed name of first witness to will.

D. Typed or printed name of second witness to will.

E. Signature of person who executed will.

F. Signature of first witness to will.

G. Signature of second witness to will.

H. Typed or printed name of person who executed will.

I. Typed or printed name of first witness to will.

J. Typed or printed name of second witness to will.

K. Date acknowledgments taken.

L. Month acknowledgments taken.

M. Year acknowledgments taken.

N. Notary's signature.

O. Date and month notary's commission expires.

P. Year notary's commission expires.

---

59. *Id.*

STATE OF NORTH CAROLINA
COUNTY/CITY OF _____(A)_____

    Before me, the undersigned authority, on this day
personally appeared _____(B)_____, _____(C)_____,
and _____(D)_____, known to me to be the testator
and the witnesses, respectively, whose names are
signed to the attached or foregoing instrument, and
all of these persons being by me first duly sworn.
The testator declared to me and to the witnesses in
my presence: that said instrument is his last will;
that he had willingly signed or directed another to
sign the same for him, and executed it in the presence of said witnesses as his free and voluntary act
for the purposes therein expressed; or that the testator signified that the instrument was his instrument
by acknowledging to them his signature previously
affixed thereto.
    The said witnesses stated before me that the
foregoing will was executed and acknowledged by the
testator as his last will in the presence of said
witnesses who, in his presence and at his request,
subscribed their names thereto as attesting witnesses
and that the testator, at the time of the execution
of said will, was over the age of 18 years and of
sound and disposing mind and memory.

                          _____(E)_____
                                   Testator
                          _____(F)_____
                                   Witness
                          _____(G)_____
                                   Witness

Subscribed, sworn to and acknowledged before me by
_____(H)_____, the testator, and subscribed and
sworn to before me by _____(I)_____ and
_____(J)_____, witnesses, this __(K)__ day of
_____(L)___, 19 (M) .

(Official Seal)   _____(N)_____
                                 Notary Public

My commission expires _____(O)_____, 19 (P) .

Example: On March 3, 1991, Julia Beard executed her will, with James ▶
Claiborne and Pierre Lee as witnesses. She decides to convert her will to a
self-proving one, and on July 1, 1992, Beard, Claiborne, and Lee appear
before Judith Fisher, a Durham County notary, to make the required acknowledgments. Fisher's commission expires July 2, 1994. The acknowledgments are taken in Durham.

STATE OF NORTH CAROLINA
COUNTY/CITY OF _____Durham_____

Before me, the undersigned authority, on this day
personally appeared ___Julia Beard___, ___James Claiborne___,
and ___Pierre Lee___, known to me to be the testator
and the witnesses, respectively, whose names are
signed to the attached or foregoing instrument, and
all of these persons being by me first duly sworn.
The testator declared to me and to the witnesses in
my presence: that said instrument is her last will;
that she had willingly signed or directed another to
sign the same for her, and executed it in the presence of said witnesses as her free and voluntary act
for the purposes therein expressed; or that the testator signified that the instrument was her instrument
by acknowledging to them her signature previously
affixed thereto.

The said witnesses stated before me that the
foregoing will was executed and acknowledged by the
testator as her last will in the presence of said
witnesses who, in her presence and at her request,
subscribed their names thereto as attesting witnesses
and that the testator, at the time of the execution
of said will, was over the age of 18 years and of
sound and disposing mind and memory.

_____
                   Testator

_____
                   Witness

_____
                   Witness

Subscribed, sworn to and acknowledged before me by
___Julia Beard___, the testator, and subscribed and
sworn to before me by __James Claiborne__ and
___Pierre Lee___, witnesses, this __1st__ day of
___July___, 19_92_ .

(Official Seal)

_____
                   Notary Public

My commission expires _____July 2_____, 19_94_ .

Living wills ▶

G.S. 90-321 provides a means by which a person may state in writing his or her wish that in the event of a terminal or incurable illness extraordinary efforts not be used to prolong his or her life. The document for this is a Declaration of a Desire for a Natural Death, popularly called a living will. The declaration must be certified, and a notary is one of the officers who may certify it. Note that both the declarant and the witnesses must be placed under oath.

A. Typed or printed name of notary.

B. Name of county where notary is commissioned.

C. Typed or printed name of person signing the declaration.

D. Typed or printed name of first witness.

E. Typed or printed name of second witness.

F. Typed or printed name of person signing the declaration.

G. Date certification made.

H. Month and year certification made.

I. Notary's signature.

J. Name of county where notary is commissioned.

K. Date and month notary's commission expires.

L. Year notary's commission expires.

Certificate

I, _____(A)_____ , Notary Public for _____(B)_____ County, hereby certify that _____(C)_____ , the declarant, appeared before me and swore to me and to the witnesses in my presence that this instrument is his Declaration Of A Desire For A Natural Death, and he willingly and voluntarily made and executed it as his free act and deed for the purposes expressed in it.

I further certify that _____(D)_____ and _____(E)_____ , witnesses, appeared before me and swore that they witnessed _____(F)_____ , declarant, sign the attached declaration, believing him to be of sound mind; and also swore that at the time they witnessed the declaration (i) they were not related within the third degree to the declarant or to the declarant's spouse, (ii) they did not know or have a reasonable expectation that they would be entitled to any portion of the estate of the declarant upon the declarant's death under any will of the declarant or codicil thereto then existing or under the Intestate Succession Act as it provides at that time, (iii) they were not a physician attending the declarant or an employee of an attending physician or an employee of a health facility in which the declarant was a patient or an employee of a nursing home or a group-care home in which the declarant resided, and (iv) they did not have a claim against the declarant. I further certify that I am satisfied as to the genuineness and due execution of the declaration.

This the __(G)__ day of _____(H)_____ .

(Official Seal)   _____(I)_____
                         Notary Public
                         for the County of _____(J)_____

My commission expires _____(K)_____ , 19_(L)_ .

Certificate

I,___Kitty Kelly___, Notary Public for ___Watauga___ County, hereby certify that ___John Hondo___, the declarant, appeared before me and swore to me and to the witnesses in my presence that this instrument is his Declaration Of A Desire For A Natural Death, and he willingly and voluntarily made and executed it as his free act and deed for the purposes expressed in it.

I further certify that ___Jack Meany___ and ___Matt Irons___, witnesses, appeared before me and swore that they witnessed ___John Hondo___, declarant, sign the attached declaration, believing him to be of sound mind; and also swore that at the time they witnessed the declaration (i) they were not related within the third degree to the declarant or to the declarant's spouse, (ii) they did not know or have a reasonable expectation that they would be entitled to any portion of the estate of the declarant upon the declarant's death under any will of the declarant or codicil thereto then existing or under the Intestate Succession Act as it provides at that time, (iii) they were not a physician attending the declarant or an employee of an attending physician or an employee of a health facility in which the declarant was a patient or an employee of a nursing home or a group-care home in which the declarant resided, and (iv) they did not have a claim against the declarant. I further certify that I am satisfied as to the genuineness and due execution of the declaration.

This the __5th__ day of ___March, 1991___.

(Official Seal)   ___Kitty Kelly___
                    Notary Public
                    for the County of ___Watauga___

My commission expires ___April 15___, 19_92_.

Example: On March 5, 1991, John Hondo signs a Declaration of a Desire for a Natural Death in the presence of Jack Meany and Matt Irons, witnesses. The certification is made before a Watauga County notary, Kitty Kelly. Kelly's commission expires April 15, 1992. The certificate is made in Boone.

Motor Vehicle Titles

Notaries frequently certify the execution of applications to transfer the title of a motor vehicle or of applications for a new title. Several general principles apply to motor vehicle certifications, no matter which of the four Division of Motor Vehicles (DMV) forms is used:

(1) Be especially careful not to make any spelling or other errors.

(2) If an error is made, do not erase it or white it out; draw one line through the error and then correct it above or to the side of the error.

(3) Be certain that *all* blanks for buyer's and seller's names and addresses, odometer readings, and similar information are filled in before taking the certification.

(4) Administer the oath to the person making the certification (G.S. 20-112 provides that making a false statement under oath with regard to motor vehicle title documents is punishable as perjury).

(5) Require *full* printed names and signatures, just as they appear on the reverse side of the title. This means that a person's middle name must be included; women should provide their given name, maiden surname or middle name, and last name.

(6) Do not use titles such as "Mr.," "Mrs.," "Ms.," "Dr.," etc.

(7) If the person whose certification is being taken has no middle name, indicate this fact by inserting the letters "NMN" in the place for a middle name.

▼ Form I

Federal and State law requires that you state the mileage in connection with the transfer of ownership. Failure to complete or providing a false statement may result in fines and/or imprisonment.

A   **ASSIGNMENT OF TITLE BY REGISTERED OWNER**

The undersigned hereby certifies that the vehicle described in this title has been transferred to the following printed name and address:

"I certify to the best of my knowledge that the odometer reading is: _____ (NO TENTHS) and reflects the actual mileage of this vehicle unless one of the following statements is checked.

☐ 1. The mileage stated is in excess of its mechanical limits.
☐ 2. The odometer reading is not the actual mileage.   **WARNING—ODOMETER DISCREPANCY**

To my knowledge the vehicle described herein ☐ has been ☐ has not been involved in collision or other

DATE VEHICLE DELIVERED TO PURCHASER   occurrence to the extent that the cost to repair exceeds 25% of fair market retail value.

Hand Printed Name and
Signature(s) of Seller(s) _____

Subscribed and Sworn to before me in my presence this _____ day of _____, 19 _____ County _____ State _____

Notary Public _____ My Commission expires the _____ day of _____, 19 _____
(SEAL)

"I am aware of the above odometer certification and damage disclosure made by the seller."

Hand Printed Name and
Signature(s) of Buyer(s) _____

B   **FIRST RE-ASSIGNMENT BY DEALER**

The undersigned hereby certifies that the vehicle described in this title has been transferred to the following printed name and address:

"I certify to the best of my knowledge that the odometer reading is: _____ (NO TENTHS) and reflects the actual mileage of this vehicle unless one of the following statements is checked.

☐ 1. The mileage stated is in excess of its mechanical limits.
☐ 2. The odometer reading is not the actual mileage.   **WARNING—ODOMETER DISCREPANCY**

To my knowledge the vehicle described herein ☐ has been ☐ has not been involved in collision or other

DATE VEHICLE DELIVERED TO PURCHASER   occurrence to the extent that the cost to repair exceeds 25% of fair market retail value.

Hand Printed Name and
Signature of Dealer or Agent _____ Dealer's No. _____

Printed Firm Name _____

Subscribed and Sworn to before me in my presence this _____ day of _____, 19 _____ County _____ State _____

Notary Public _____ My Commission expires the _____ day of _____, 19 _____
(SEAL)

"I am aware of the above odometer certification and damage disclosure made by the seller."

Hand Printed Name and
Signature(s) of Buyer(s) _____

C   **PURCHASER'S APPLICATION FOR NEW CERTIFICATE OF TITLE**

THE UNDERSIGNED, PURCHASER OF THE VEHICLE DESCRIBED ON THE FACE OF THIS CERTIFICATE, HEREBY MAKES APPLICATION FOR A NEW CERTIFICATE OF TITLE AND CERTIFIES THAT SAID VEHICLE IS SUBJECT TO THE FOLLOWING NAMED LIENS AND NONE OTHER, AND THAT THE INFORMATION CONTAINED HEREIN IS TRUE AND ACCURATE TO MY BEST KNOWLEDGE AND BELIEF.

OWNER'S CERTIFICATION FOR ELIGIBILITY TO REGISTER	FIRST LIEN	DATE _____
I CERTIFY FOR THE MOTOR VEHICLE DESCRIBED ON THIS TITLE THAT: 1. I HAVE FINANCIAL RESPONSIBILITY AS REQUIRED BY LAW.	LIENHOLDER	
Print or type full name of insurance company licensed in N.C.—not agency or group	STREET OR R.F.D	CITY OR TOWN
Policy number—If policy not issued, name of agency binding coverage 2. I OWE NO DELINQUENT COUNTY OR MUNICIPAL TAXES ON THIS VEHICLE. 3. I WAS THE LEGAL OWNER OF THIS VEHICLE ON JANUARY 1ST OF THE YEAR OF THIS APPLICATION AND THE VEHICLE WAS LISTED FOR PROPERTY TAXES	SECOND LIEN	DATE _____
IN _____ IN _____ (County) (Month) (Year) 4. I WAS NOT THE LEGAL OWNER OF THIS VEHICLE ON JANUARY 1ST OF THE YEAR OF THIS APPLICATION ☐ (Check Block)	LIENHOLDER STREET OR R.F.D CITY OR TOWN	

SIGNATURE OF PURCHASER(S)

	Purchase Price	Odometer Reading (No Tenths)
	$	

FIRST NAME   MIDDLE NAME   LAST NAME

ALL ANSWERS SUPPLIED AND COMPLETELY SUBSCRIBED AND SWORN TO BEFORE

ME THIS _____ DAY OF _____ 19 _____

MY COMMISSION EXPIRES _____

PRINT IN INK OR TYPE NAME EXACTLY AS IT APPEARS ABOVE IN SIGNATURE

_____ (SEAL)

RESIDENCE ADDRESS   SIGNATURE OF NOTARY PUBLIC IN INK

POST OFFICE   COUNTY OF RESIDENCE   ZIP CODE   ADDRESS OF NOTARY PUBLIC

NOTE: RETAIL PURCHASER MUST APPLY FOR NEW TITLE WITHIN 20 DAYS AFTER PURCHASE OR PAY STATUTORY PENALTY. ALTERATIONS OR ERASURES WILL VOID THIS TITLE

(Form I) Part A. Assignment of Title by Registered Owner

Federal and State law requires that you state the mileage in connection with the transfer of ownership. Failure to complete or providing a false statement may result in fines and/or imprisonment.

A

ASSIGNMENT OF TITLE BY REGISTERED OWNER

The undersigned hereby certifies that the vehicle described in this title has been transferred to the following printed name and address:

Ⓐ   Ⓑ

"I certify to the best of my knowledge that the odometer reading is: _____ Ⓒ _____ **(NO TENTHS)** and reflects the actual mileage of this vehicle unless one of the following statements is checked.

☐ 1. The mileage stated is in excess of its mechanical limits.
☐ 2. The odometer reading is not the actual mileage.   **WARNING—ODOMETER DISCREPANCY**

Ⓓ
DATE VEHICLE DELIVERED TO PURCHASER   To my knowledge the vehicle described herein ☐ has been ☐ has not been involved in collision or other occurrence to the extent that the cost to repair exceeds 25% of fair market retail value.

Hand Printed Name and
Signature(s) of Seller(s) _____ Ⓔ _____ Ⓕ _____

Subscribed and Sworn to before me in my presence this __ Ⓖ __ day of __ Ⓗ __ 19 Ⓘ __ County _____ Ⓙ _____ State __ Ⓚ __

Notary Public _____ Ⓛ _____ My Commission expires the Ⓜ __ day of Ⓝ __ 19 Ⓞ
(SEAL)

"I am aware of the above odometer certification and damage disclosure made by the seller."

Hand Printed Name and
Signature(s) of Buyer(s) _____ Ⓟ _____ Ⓠ _____

B   **FIRST RE-ASSIGNMENT BY DEALER**

A. Full typed or printed name of purchaser.
B. Purchaser's street or box address and city or town.
C. Vehicle's odometer reading on date assignment of title is executed.
D. Date vehicle delivered to purchaser (usually date of title assignment).
E. Seller's full hand-printed name.
F. Seller's full signature.
G. Date notary takes certification.
H. Month notary takes certification.

I. Year notary takes certification.
J. County where assignment executed.
K. State where assignment executed.
L. Notary's signature as it appears in the seal or stamp.
M. Date notary's commission expires.
N. Month notary's commission expires.
O. Year notary's commission expires.
P. Buyer's full hand-printed name.
Q. Buyer's full signature.

Federal and State law requires that you state the mileage in connection with the transfer of ownership. Failure to complete or providing a false statement may result in fines and/or imprisonment.

A

ASSIGNMENT OF TITLE BY REGISTERED OWNER

The undersigned hereby certifies that the vehicle described in this title has been transferred to the following printed name and address:

Friendly Used Cars, 123 Main Drag, Burgaw

"I certify to the best of my knowledge that the odometer reading is: _____ 41060 _____ **(NO TENTHS)** and reflects the actual mileage of this vehicle unless one of the following statements is checked.

☐ 1. The mileage stated is in excess of its mechanical limits.
☐ 2. The odometer reading is not the actual mileage.   **WARNING—ODOMETER DISCREPANCY**

4/1/91
DATE VEHICLE DELIVERED TO PURCHASER   To my knowledge the vehicle described herein ☐ has been ☐ has not been involved in collision or other occurrence to the extent that the cost to repair exceeds 25% of fair market retail value.

Hand Printed Name and
Signature(s) of Seller(s) Cary Joe Simpson   Cary Joe Simpson

Subscribed and Sworn to before me in my presence this 1st day of April 19 91 County Pender State NC

Notary Public Michael X. Soileau   My Commission expires the 10th day of June 19 93
(SEAL)

"I am aware of the above odometer certification and damage disclosure made by the seller."

Hand Printed Name and
Signature(s) of Buyer(s) Friendly Used Cars by Otto Wanton

B   **FIRST RE-ASSIGNMENT BY DEALER**

(Form I) Part B. Reassignment of Title by Registered Dealer

Hand Printed Name and Signature(s) of Buyer(s) _____

B | **FIRST RE-ASSIGNMENT BY DEALER**

The undersigned hereby certifies that the vehicle described in this title has been transferred to the following printed name and address:

Ⓐ Ⓒ

"I certify to the best of my knowledge that the odometer reading is: _____ **(NO TENTHS)** and reflects the actual mileage of this vehicle unless one of the following statements is checked.

☐ 1. The mileage stated is in excess of its mechanical limits.
☐ 2. The odometer reading is not the actual mileage.   **WARNING—ODOMETER DISCREPANCY**

Ⓓ   To my knowledge the vehicle described herein ☐ has been ☐ has not been involved in collision or other

DATE VEHICLE DELIVERED TO PURCHASER   occurrence to the extent that the cost to repair exceeds 25% of fair market retail value.

Hand Printed Name and Signature of Dealer or Agent _____ Ⓔ _____ Ⓕ _____ Dealer's No. Ⓖ

Printed Firm Name Ⓗ

Subscribed and Sworn to before me in my presence this Ⓘ day of Ⓙ 19 Ⓚ County Ⓛ State Ⓜ

Notary Public _____ Ⓝ _____ My Commission expires the Ⓞ day of Ⓟ 19 Ⓠ
(SEAL)

"I am aware of the above odometer certification and damage disclosure made by the seller."

Hand Printed Name and Signature(s) of Buyer(s) _____ Ⓡ _____ Ⓢ

C | **PURCHASER'S APPLICATION FOR NEW CERTIFICATE OF TITLE**

A. Full typed or printed name of purchaser.	H. Full printed or typed name of dealer.
B. Purchaser's street or box address and city or town.	I. Date notary takes certification.
C. Vehicle's odometer reading at date of title reassignment.	J. Month notary takes certification.
	K. Year notary takes certification.
D. Date vehicle delivered by dealer to new owner (usually date of title reassignment).	L. County where reassignment is executed.
	M. State where reassignment is executed.
E. Full hand-printed name of agent signing for dealership.	N. Notary's signature as it appears in the seal or stamp.
F. Full signature of dealer's agent (omission of this item will cause title application to be rejected).	O. Date notary's commission expires.
	P. Month notary's commission expires.
	Q. Year notary's commission expires.
G. Dealer's certificate number.	R. Buyer's full hand-printed name.
	S. Buyer's full signature.

Hand Printed Name and Signature(s) of Buyer(s) _Friendly Used Cars by Otto Wanton_

B | **FIRST RE-ASSIGNMENT BY DEALER**

The undersigned hereby certifies that the vehicle described in this title has been transferred to the following printed name and address:

Bobby Wayne King, RR 1, Box 750, Burgaw

"I certify to the best of my knowledge that the odometer reading is: _41141_ **(NO TENTHS)** and reflects the actual mileage of this vehicle unless one of the following statements is checked.

☐ 1. The mileage stated is in excess of its mechanical limits.
☐ 2. The odometer reading is not the actual mileage.   **WARNING—ODOMETER DISCREPANCY**

_5/1/91_   To my knowledge the vehicle described herein ☐ has been ☒ has not been involved in collision or other

DATE VEHICLE DELIVERED TO PURCHASER   occurrence to the extent that the cost to repair exceeds 25% of fair market retail value.

Hand Printed Name and Signature of Dealer or Agent _Michele Morris_ _Michele Morris_ _____ Dealer's No. _51056_

Printed Firm Name _Friendly Used Cars_

Subscribed and Sworn to before me in my presence this _1st_ day of _May_ 19 _91_ County _Pender_ State _NC_

Notary Public _Diantha McGeachy_ _____ My Commission expires the _15th_ day of _July_ 19 _94_
(SEAL)

"I am aware of the above odometer certification and damage disclosure made by the seller."

Hand Printed Name and Signature(s) of Buyer(s) _Bobby Wayne King_ _Bobby Wayne King_

C | **PURCHASER'S APPLICATION FOR NEW CERTIFICATE OF TITLE**

(Form I) Part C. Purchaser's Application for New Certificate of Title

PURCHASER'S APPLICATION FOR NEW CERTIFICATE OF TITLE

THE UNDERSIGNED, PURCHASER OF THE VEHICLE DESCRIBED ON THE FACE OF THIS CERTIFICATE, HEREBY MAKES APPLICATION FOR A NEW CERTIFICATE OF TITLE AND CERTIFIES THAT SAID VEHICLE IS SUBJECT TO THE FOLLOWING NAMED LIENS AND NONE OTHER, AND THAT THE INFORMATION CONTAINED HEREIN IS TRUE AND ACCURATE TO MY BEST KNOWLEDGE AND BELIEF.

OWNER'S CERTIFICATION FOR ELIGIBILITY TO REGISTER
I CERTIFY FOR THE MOTOR VEHICLE DESCRIBED ON THIS TITLE THAT:
I HAVE FINANCIAL RESPONSIBILITY AS REQUIRED BY LAW.

(A)

Print or type full name of insurance company licensed in N.C.—not agency or group

(B)

Policy number—If policy not issued, name of agency binding coverage

I OWE NO DELINQUENT COUNTY OR MUNICIPAL TAXES ON THIS VEHICLE.
I WAS THE LEGAL OWNER OF THIS VEHICLE ON JANUARY 1ST OF THE YEAR OF THIS APPLICATION AND THE VEHICLE WAS LISTED FOR PROPERTY TAXES.

N **(C)** IN **(D)** **(E)**
(County) (Month) (Year)

I WAS NOT THE LEGAL OWNER OF THIS VEHICLE ON JANUARY 1ST OF THE YEAR OF THIS APPLICATION ☐
(Check Block)

FIRST LIEN DATE **(F)**

LIENHOLDER **(G)** **(H)** **(I)**

STREET OR R.F.D. CITY OR TOWN

SECOND LIEN DATE

LIENHOLDER

STREET OR R.F.D. CITY OR TOWN

SIGNATURE OF PURCHASER(S)

(J)

FIRST NAME MIDDLE NAME LAST NAME

(K)
(L)

PRINT IN INK OR TYPE NAME EXACTLY AS IT APPEARS ABOVE IN SIGNATURE

RESIDENCE ADDRESS **(M)** **(N)** **(O)**

POST OFFICE COUNTY OF RESIDENCE ZIP CODE

Purchase Price **(P)** Odometer Reading (No Tenths) **(Q)**
$

ALL ANSWERS SUPPLIED AND COMPLETELY SUBSCRIBED AND SWORN TO BEFORE **(T)**
ME THIS **(R)** DAY OF **(S)** **(U)** 19___

MY COMMISSION EXPIRES **(V)**
_____ (SEAL)

SIGNATURE OF NOTARY PUBLIC IN INK **(W)**

ADDRESS OF NOTARY PUBLIC

NOTE: RETAIL PURCHASER MUST APPLY FOR NEW TITLE WITHIN 20 DAYS AFTER PURCHASE OR PAY STATUTORY PENALTY. ALTERATIONS OR ERASURES WILL VOID THIS TITLE

A. Full typed or printed name of insurance company issuing policy that insures vehicle.

B. Insurance policy number.

C. County in which vehicle was listed for property taxes for current year.

D. Month vehicle was listed for taxes.

E. Year vehicle was listed for taxes.

F. Date of creation of first lien.

G. Name of holder of first lien on vehicle purchased.

H. Lienholder's street or box address.

I. Lienholder's address, city, or town.

J. Owner's full signature.

K. Full typed or printed name of owner exactly as it appears on the signature line.

L. Owner's street address.

M. Owner's city or town.

N. Owner's county of residence.

O. Owner's zip code.

P. Amount purchaser paid for vehicle.

Q. Odometer reading of vehicle on date application is signed.

R. Date notary takes certification.

S. Month notary takes certification.

T. Year notary takes certification.

U. Date, month, and year notary's commission expires.

V. Notary's signature as it appears in the seal or stamp.

W. Notary's address, city, and state.

▼ *Example*: Cary Joe Simpson sells his 1987 Buick to Friendly Used Cars. Friendly sells the car to Bobby Wayne King, and King applies for a new certificate of title in his name. The transactions are all certified before different Pender County notaries, but all take place in the town of Burgaw.

C   PURCHASER'S APPLICATION FOR NEW CERTIFICATE OF TITLE

THE UNDERSIGNED, PURCHASER OF THE VEHICLE DESCRIBED ON THE FACE OF THIS CERTIFICATE, HEREBY MAKES APPLICATION FOR A NEW CERTIFICATE OF TITLE AND CERTIFIES THAT SAID VEHICLE IS SUBJECT TO THE FOLLOWING NAMED LIENS AND NONE OTHER, AND THAT THE INFORMATION CONTAINED HEREIN IS TRUE AND ACCURATE TO MY BEST KNOWLEDGE AND BELIEF.

OWNER'S CERTIFICATION FOR ELIGIBILITY TO REGISTER
I CERTIFY FOR THE MOTOR VEHICLE DESCRIBED ON THIS TITLE THAT:
1. I HAVE FINANCIAL RESPONSIBILITY AS REQUIRED BY LAW.
   Allfarm Automobile Insurance Company
   Print or type full name of insurance company licensed in N.C.—not agency or group
   F-416-C04-H2C06
   Policy number—If policy not issued, name of agency binding coverage
2. I OWE NO DELINQUENT COUNTY OR MUNICIPAL TAXES ON THIS VEHICLE.
3. I WAS THE LEGAL OWNER OF THIS VEHICLE ON JANUARY 1ST OF THE YEAR OF THIS APPLICATION AND THE VEHICLE WAS LISTED FOR PROPERTY TAXES

IN _____ IN _____ IN _____
   (County)   (Month)   (Year)
4. I WAS NOT THE LEGAL OWNER OF THIS VEHICLE ON JANUARY 1ST OF THE YEAR OF THIS APPLICATION   X
   (Check Block)

FIRST LIEN   DATE 5/1/91
First Village Automobile Bank
LIENHOLDER
202 Witherspoon Rd., Burgaw
STREET OR R.F.D.   CITY OR TOWN

SECOND LIEN   DATE _____
LIENHOLDER
STREET OR R.F.D.   CITY OR TOWN

SIGNATURE OF PURCHASER(S)

Bobby Wayne King
FIRST NAME   MIDDLE NAME   LAST NAME

Bobby Wayne King
PRINT IN INK OR TYPE NAME EXACTLY AS IT APPEARS ABOVE IN SIGNATURE
R.R.1, Box 750
RESIDENCE ADDRESS
Burgaw   Pender   28240
POST OFFICE   COUNTY OF RESIDENCE   ZIP CODE

Purchase Price	Odometer Reading (No Tenths)
4,800	41141

ALL ANSWERS SUPPLIED AND COMPLETELY SUBSCRIBED AND SWORN TO BEFORE
ME THIS 1st DAY OF May 19 91
MY COMMISSION EXPIRES September 21, 1994
Elizabeth Penner (SEAL)
SIGNATURE OF NOTARY PUBLIC IN INK
4-U Ritten Rd., Burgaw, N.C.
ADDRESS OF NOTARY PUBLIC

NOTE: RETAIL PURCHASER MUST APPLY FOR NEW TITLE WITHIN 20 DAYS AFTER PURCHASE OR PAY STATUTORY PENALTY. ALTERATIONS OR ERASURES WILL VOID THIS TITLE

▼ Form II

Form II is a title certificate that has been in use for several years. Note that in Part A of this form the notary is taking the acknowledgment of the seller only.

A ASSIGNMENT OF TITLE BY REGISTERED OWNER

FOR VALUE RECEIVED, THE UNDERSIGNED HEREBY SELLS, ASSIGNS OR TRANSFERS THE VEHICLE DESCRIBED ON THE REVERSE SIDE OF THIS CERTIFICATE UNTO THE PURCHASER WHOSE NAME APPEARS IN THIS BLOCK AND HEREBY WARRANTS THE TITLE TO SAID VEHICLE AND CERTIFIES THAT AT THE TIME OF DELIVERY THE SAME IS SUBJECT TO THE LIENS OR ENCUMBRANCES NAMED IN THE PURCHASER'S APPLICATION FOR NEW CERTIFICATE OF TITLE AND NONE OTHER.

PURCHASER'S FIRST, MIDDLE AND LAST NAMES (PRINT IN INK OR TYPE)   STREET OR R.F.D.   CITY OR TOWN

(FEDERAL AND STATE REGULATIONS REQUIRE YOU TO STATE THE ODOMETER MILEAGE UPON TRANSFER OF OWNERSHIP (G. S. 20-347).)

I CERTIFY TO THE BEST OF MY KNOWLEDGE THAT THE ODOMETER READING IS   Odometer Reading   AND REFLECTS THE ACTUAL
MILEAGE OF THE VEHICLE UNLESS ONE OR MORE OF THE FOLLOWING STATE-   MENTS IS CHECKED
☐ 1. THE AMOUNT OF MILEAGE STATED IS IN EXCESS OF 99,999 MILES OR
☐ 2. THE ODOMETER READING IS NOT THE ACTUAL MILEAGE AND SHOULD NOT BE RELIED UPON.
☐ 3. THE ODOMETER WAS ALTERED FOR REPAIR OR REPLACEMENT PURPOSES BY _____
ON _____ AND APPROXIMATELY _____ MILES WERE REMOVED BY THE ALTERATION.

PURCHASER'S SIGNATURE
(CONFIRMING ODOMETER READING ONLY)   DATE VEHICLE DELIVERED TO PURCHASER

ALL ANSWERS SUPPLIED AND ACKNOWLEDGED BEFORE ME

SELLER'S SIGNATURE   THIS _____ DAY OF _____ 19 _____

MY COMMISSION EXPIRES _____

_____ (SEAL)
SIGNATURE OF NOTARY PUBLIC IN INK

B PURCHASER'S APPLICATION FOR NEW CERTIFICATE OF TITLE

THE UNDERSIGNED, PURCHASER OF THE VEHICLE DESCRIBED ON THE FACE OF THIS CERTIFICATE, HEREBY MAKES APPLICATION FOR A NEW CERTIFICATE OF TITLE AND CERTIFIES THAT SAID VEHICLE IS SUBJECT TO THE FOLLOWING NAMED LIENS AND NONE OTHER, AND THAT THE INFORMATION CONTAINED HEREIN IS TRUE AND ACCURATE TO MY BEST KNOWLEDGE AND BELIEF.

OWNER'S CERTIFICATION FOR ELIGIBILITY TO REGISTER

I CERTIFY FOR THE MOTOR VEHICLE DESCRIBED ON THIS TITLE THAT
1. I HAVE FINANCIAL RESPONSIBILITY AS REQUIRED BY LAW

Print or type full name of insurance company licensed in N.C.—not agency or group

Policy number—If policy not issued, name of agent binding coverage
2. I OWE NO DELINQUENT COUNTY OR MUNICIPAL TAXES ON THIS VEHICLE
3. I WAS THE LEGAL OWNER OF THIS VEHICLE ON JANUARY 1ST OF THE YEAR OF THIS APPLICATION AND THE VEHICLE WAS LISTED FOR PROPERTY TAXES

in _____ in _____ _____
(County)   (Month)   (Year)
4. I WAS NOT THE LEGAL OWNER OF THIS VEHICLE ON JANUARY 1ST OF THE YEAR OF THIS APPLICATION
(Check Block)

FIRST LIEN   DATE _____

LIENHOLDER

STREET OR R.F.D.   CITY OR TOWN

SECOND LIEN   DATE _____

LIENHOLDER

STREET OR R.F.D.   CITY OR TOWN

SIGNATURE OF OWNER(S) IN INK FOR TITLE, AD VALOREM TAX, AND INSURANCE CERTIFICATION

5.
FIRST NAME   MIDDLE NAME   LAST NAME   PLATE TO BE TRANSFERRED   GROSS WEIGHT   ODOMETER READING

ALL ANSWERS SUPPLIED AND ACKNOWLEDGED BEFORE ME

6.
PRINT IN INK OR TYPE NAME EXACTLY AS IT APPEARS ABOVE IN SIGNATURE   THIS _____ DAY OF _____ 19 _____

MY COMMISSION EXPIRES _____

7.
RESIDENCE ADDRESS   SIGNATURE OF NOTARY PUBLIC IN INK

8.
POST OFFICE   COUNTY OF RESIDENCE   ZIP CODE   ADDRESS OF NOTARY PUBLIC   (SEAL)

(Dealer Reassignment must be made on form MVR-2)

NOTE: RETAIL PURCHASER MUST APPLY FOR NEW TITLE WITHIN 20 DAYS AFTER PURCHASE OR PAY STATUTORY PENALTY

LIEN OR ENCUMBRANCE—ENTER IN SECTION B

ALTERATIONS OR ERASURES WILL VOID THIS TITLE

VOID

(Form II) Part A. Assignment of Title by Registered Owner

ASSIGNMENT OF TITLE BY REGISTERED OWNER

FOR VALUE RECEIVED, THE UNDERSIGNED HEREBY SELLS, ASSIGNS OR TRANSFERS THE VEHICLE DESCRIBED ON THE REVERSE SIDE OF THIS CERTIFICATE UNTO THE PURCHASER WHOSE NAME APPEARS IN THIS BLOCK AND HEREBY WARRANTS THE TITLE TO SAID VEHICLE AND CERTIFIES THAT AT THE TIME OF DELIVERY THE SAME IS SUBJECT TO THE LIENS OR ENCUMBRANCES NAMED IN THE PURCHASER'S APPLICATION FOR NEW CERTIFICATE OF TITLE AND NONE OTHER.

PURCHASER'S FIRST, MIDDLE AND LAST NAMES (PRINT IN INK OR TYPE)   STREET OR R.F.D.   CITY OR TOWN

(FEDERAL AND STATE REGULATIONS REQUIRE YOU TO STATE THE ODOMETER MILEAGE UPON TRANSFER OF OWNERSHIP (G. S. 20-347).)

I CERTIFY TO THE BEST OF MY KNOWLEDGE THAT THE ODOMETER READING IS | Odometer Reading | AND REFLECTS THE ACTUAL MILEAGE OF THE VEHICLE UNLESS ONE OR MORE OF THE FOLLOWING STATE-   MENTS IS CHECKED.
☐ 1. THE AMOUNT OF MILEAGE STATED IS IN EXCESS OF 99,999 MILES OR
☐ 2. THE ODOMETER READING IS NOT THE ACTUAL MILEAGE AND SHOULD NOT BE RELIED UPON.
☐ 3. THE ODOMETER WAS ALTERED FOR REPAIR OR REPLACEMENT PURPOSES BY

ON _____ AND APPROXIMATELY _____ MILES WERE REMOVED BY THE ALTERATION.

PURCHASER'S SIGNATURE (CONFIRMING ODOMETER READING ONLY)   DATE VEHICLE DELIVERED TO PURCHASER

ALL ANSWERS SUPPLIED AND ACKNOWLEDGED BEFORE ME

SELLER'S SIGNATURE

THIS _____ DAY OF _____ 19 ___

MY COMMISSION EXPIRES _____

SIGNATURE OF NOTARY PUBLIC IN INK _____ (SEAL)

PURCHASER'S APPLICATION FOR NEW CERTIFICATE OF TITLE

(left margin) YS AFTER PURCHASE OR PAY STATUTORY PENALTY
(right margin) EN OR ENCUMBRANCE—ENTER IN SECTION B

A. Full typed or printed name of purchaser.

B. Purchaser's street or box address.

C. Purchaser's city or town.

D. Vehicle's odometer reading on date assignment of title is executed.

E. Purchaser's full signature.

F. Date vehicle delivered to purchaser (usually date of title assignment).

G. Seller's full signature.

H. Date notary takes certification.

I. Month notary takes certification.

J. Year notary takes certification.

K. Date, month, and year notary's commission expires.

L. Notary's signature as it appears in the seal or stamp.

ASSIGNMENT OF TITLE BY REGISTERED OWNER

FOR VALUE RECEIVED, THE UNDERSIGNED HEREBY SELLS, ASSIGNS OR TRANSFERS THE VEHICLE DESCRIBED ON THE REVERSE SIDE OF THIS CERTIFICATE UNTO THE PURCHASER WHOSE NAME APPEARS IN THIS BLOCK AND HEREBY WARRANTS THE TITLE TO SAID VEHICLE AND CERTIFIES THAT AT THE TIME OF DELIVERY THE SAME IS SUBJECT TO THE LIENS OR ENCUMBRANCES NAMED IN THE PURCHASER'S APPLICATION FOR NEW CERTIFICATE OF TITLE AND NONE OTHER

Calvin Coolidge Whitley   2 Spring St.   Roxboro

PURCHASER'S FIRST, MIDDLE AND LAST NAMES (PRINT IN INK OR TYPE)   STREET OR R.F.D.   CITY OR TOWN

(FEDERAL AND STATE REGULATIONS REQUIRE YOU TO STATE THE ODOMETER MILEAGE UPON TRANSFER OF OWNERSHIP (G. S. 20-347).)

I CERTIFY TO THE BEST OF MY KNOWLEDGE THAT THE ODOMETER READING IS | Odometer Reading **24060** | AND REFLECTS THE ACTUAL MILEAGE OF THE VEHICLE UNLESS ONE OR MORE OF THE FOLLOWING STATE-   MENTS IS CHECKED.
☐ 1. THE AMOUNT OF MILEAGE STATED IS IN EXCESS OF 99,999 MILES OR
☐ 2. THE ODOMETER READING IS NOT THE ACTUAL MILEAGE AND SHOULD NOT BE RELIED UPON.
☐ 3. THE ODOMETER WAS ALTERED FOR REPAIR OR REPLACEMENT PURPOSES BY

ON _____ AND APPROXIMATELY _____ MILES WERE REMOVED BY THE ALTERATION.

Calvin Coolidge Whitley

PURCHASER'S SIGNATURE (CONFIRMING ODOMETER READING ONLY)

8/8/92

DATE VEHICLE DELIVERED TO PURCHASER

Jefferson Jackson Rogers

SELLER'S SIGNATURE

ALL ANSWERS SUPPLIED AND ACKNOWLEDGED BEFORE ME

THIS 8th DAY OF August 19 92

MY COMMISSION EXPIRES 12/24/93

John Leland Somerville (SEAL)

SIGNATURE OF NOTARY PUBLIC IN INK

PURCHASER'S APPLICATION FOR NEW CERTIFICATE OF TITLE

(left margin) YS AFTER PURCHASE OR PAY STATUTORY PENALTY
(right margin) EN OR ENCUMBRANCE—ENTER IN SECTION B

(Form II) Part B. Purchaser's Application for New Certificate of Title

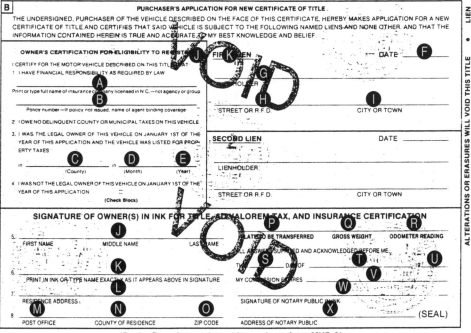

(Dealer Reassignment must be made on form MVR-2)

A. Full typed or printed name of insurance company issuing policy that insures vehicle.

B. Insurance policy number.

C. County in which vehicle was listed for property taxes for current year.

D. Month vehicle was listed for taxes.

E. Year vehicle was listed for taxes.

F. Date of creation of first lien.

G. Name of holder of first lien on vehicle purchased.

H. Lienholder's street or box address.

I. Lienholder's address, city, or town.

J. Owner's full signature.

K. Full typed or printed name of owner exactly as it appears on the signature line.

L. Owner's street address.

M. Owner's city or town.

N. Owner's county of residence.

O. Owner's zip code.

P. N.C. license plate number if it is to be transferred.

Q. Vehicle's gross weight.

R. Odometer reading of vehicle on date application is signed.

S. Date notary takes certification.

T. Month notary takes certification.

U. Year notary takes certification.

V. Date, month, and year notary's commission expires.

W. Notary's signature as it appears in the seal or stamp.

X. Notary's address, city, and state.

▼ *Example*: Jefferson Jackson Rogers sells his 1988 Oldsmobile to Calvin Coolidge Whitley, and Whitley applies for a new title. The transactions take place in Roxboro before different Person County notaries.

B	**LIEN C**

PURCHASER'S APPLICATION FOR NEW CERTIFICATE OF TITLE.

THE UNDERSIGNED, PURCHASER OF THE VEHICLE DESCRIBED ON THE FACE OF THIS CERTIFICATE, HEREBY MAKES APPLICATION FOR A NEW CERTIFICATE OF TITLE AND CERTIFIES THAT SAID VEHICLE IS SUBJECT TO THE FOLLOWING NAMED LIENS AND NONE OTHER, AND THAT THE INFORMATION CONTAINED HEREIN IS TRUE AND ACCURATE TO MY BEST KNOWLEDGE AND BELIEF.

OWNER'S CERTIFICATION FOR ELIGIBILITY TO REGISTER

FIRST LIEN   DATE 8/11/92

I CERTIFY FOR THE MOTOR VEHICLE DESCRIBED ON THIS TITLE THAT

1. I HAVE FINANCIAL RESPONSIBILITY AS REQUIRED BY LAW   Bank of Banks, Inc.

Profiteers' Insurance Company   HOLDER

Print or type full name of insurance company licensed in N.C.—not agency or group

217-64-3568   105 Seward Place,   Roxboro

Policy number—if policy not issued, name of agent binding coverage   STREET OR R.F.D.   CITY OR TOWN

2. I OWE NO DELINQUENT COUNTY OR MUNICIPAL TAXES ON THIS VEHICLE

3. I WAS THE LEGAL OWNER OF THIS VEHICLE ON JANUARY 1ST OF THE YEAR OF THIS APPLICATION AND THE VEHICLE WAS LISTED FOR PROPERTY TAXES

SECOND LIEN   DATE _____

in _____ in _____

(County)   (Month)   (Year)   LIENHOLDER

4. I WAS NOT THE LEGAL OWNER OF THIS VEHICLE ON JANUARY 1ST OF THE YEAR OF THIS APPLICATION   X

(Check Block)   STREET OR R.F.D.   CITY OR TOWN

SIGNATURE OF OWNER(S) IN INK FOR TITLE, AD VALOREM TAX, AND INSURANCE CERTIFICATION

5. *Calvin Coolidge Whitley*   ZIPPY   4403   24814

FIRST NAME   MIDDLE NAME   LAST NAME   PLATE TO BE TRANSFERRED   GROSS WEIGHT   ODOMETER READING

ALL ANSWERS SUPPLIED AND ACKNOWLEDGED BEFORE ME,

6. **Calvin Coolidge Whitley**   THIS 11th DAY OF August 19 92

PRINT IN INK OR TYPE NAME EXACTLY AS IT APPEARS ABOVE IN SIGNATURE   MY COMMISSION EXPIRES August 15, 1992

7. **2 Spring St**   *Timothy Garrett League*

RESIDENCE ADDRESS   SIGNATURE OF NOTARY PUBLIC IN INK

8. **Roxboro**   **Person**   **27763**   54 Davie Circle, Roxboro, NC   (SEAL)

POST OFFICE   COUNTY OF RESIDENCE   ZIP CODE   ADDRESS OF NOTARY PUBLIC

(Dealer Reassignment must be made on form MVR-2)

NOTE: RETAIL PURCHASER MUST APPLY FOR NEW TITLE WITHIN 20 DAYS

ALTERATIONS OR ERASURES WILL VOID THIS TITLE

▼ Form III

Form III is a title certificate that has been in use for several years by the DMV. It consists of two sections: Part A, for the assignment of titles by the current registered owner, and Part B, for reassignment by a registered dealer. Note that in Part A the notary is taking the acknowledgment of the seller only. The purchaser's application for a new title must be made with Form IV.

A   **ASSIGNMENT OF TITLE BY REGISTERED OWNER**

FOR VALUE RECEIVED, THE UNDERSIGNED HEREBY SELLS, ASSIGNS OR TRANSFERS THE VEHICLE DESCRIBED ON THE REVERSE SIDE OF THIS CERTIFICATE UNTO THE PURCHASER WHOSE NAME APPEARS IN THIS BLOCK AND HEREBY WARRANTS THE TITLE TO SAID VEHICLE AND CERTIFIES THAT AT THE TIME OF DELIVERY THE SAME IS SUBJECT TO THE LIENS OR ENCUMBRANCES NAMED IN THE PURCHASER'S APPLICATION FOR NEW CERTIFICATE OF TITLE AND NONE OTHER.

PURCHASER'S FIRST, MIDDLE AND LAST NAMES (PRINT IN INK OR TYPE)   STREET OR R.F.D.   CITY OR TOWN

(FEDERAL AND STATE REGULATIONS REQUIRE YOU TO STATE THE ODOMETER MILEAGE UPON TRANSFER OF OWNERSHIP (G. S. 20-347).)

I CERTIFY TO THE BEST OF MY KNOWLEDGE THAT THE ODOMETER READING IS | Odometer Reading | AND REFLECTS THE ACTUAL
MILEAGE OF THE VEHICLE UNLESS ONE OR MORE OF THE FOLLOWING STATEMENTS IS CHECKED:
☐ 1. THE AMOUNT OF MILEAGE STATED IS IN EXCESS OF 99,999 MILES OR
☐ 2. THE ODOMETER READING IS NOT THE ACTUAL MILEAGE AND SHOULD NOT BE RELIED UPON.
☐ 3. THE ODOMETER WAS ALTERED FOR REPAIR OR REPLACEMENT PURPOSES BY _____

ON _____ AND APPROXIMATELY _____ MILES WERE REMOVED BY THE ALTERATION.

PURCHASER'S SIGNATURE

DATE VEHICLE DELIVERED TO PURCHASER

ALL ANSWERS SUPPLIED AND COMPLETELY SUBSCRIBED AND SWORN
TO BEFORE ME THIS _____ DAY OF _____ .
19_____

SELLER'S SIGNATURE

MY COMMISSION EXPIRES: _____

_____ (SEAL)
SIGNATURE OF NOTARY PUBLIC IN INK

B   **RE-ASSIGNMENT OF TITLE BY REGISTERED DEALER**

FOR VALUE RECEIVED, THE UNDERSIGNED HEREBY SELLS, ASSIGNS OR TRANSFERS THE VEHICLE DESCRIBED ON THE REVERSE SIDE OF THIS CERTIFICATE UNTO THE PURCHASER WHOSE NAME APPEARS IN THIS BLOCK AND HEREBY WARRANTS THE TITLE TO SAID VEHICLE AND CERTIFIES THAT AT THE TIME OF DELIVERY THE SAME IS SUBJECT TO THE LIENS OR ENCUMBRANCES NAMED IN THE PURCHASER'S APPLICATION FOR NEW CERTIFICATE OF TITLE AND NONE OTHER.

PURCHASER'S FIRST, MIDDLE AND LAST NAMES (PRINT IN INK OR TYPE)   STREET OR R.F.D.   CITY OR TOWN

(FEDERAL AND STATE REGULATIONS REQUIRE YOU TO STATE THE ODOMETER MILEAGE UPON TRANSFER OF OWNERSHIP (G. S. 20-347).)

I CERTIFY TO THE BEST OF MY KNOWLEDGE THAT THE ODOMETER READING IS | Odometer Reading | AND REFLECTS THE ACTUAL
MILEAGE OF THE VEHICLE UNLESS ONE OR MORE OF THE FOLLOWING STATEMENTS IS CHECKED:
☐ 1. THE AMOUNT OF MILEAGE STATED IS IN EXCESS OF 99,999 MILES OR
☐ 2. THE ODOMETER READING IS NOT THE ACTUAL MILEAGE AND SHOULD NOT BE RELIED UPON.
☐ 3. THE ODOMETER WAS ALTERED FOR REPAIR OR REPLACEMENT PURPOSES BY _____

ON _____ AND APPROXIMATELY _____ MILES WERE REMOVED BY THE ALTERATION.

PURCHASER'S SIGNATURE

DATE VEHICLE DELIVERED TO PURCHASER

ALL ANSWERS SUPPLIED AND COMPLETELY SUBSCRIBED AND SWORN
TO BEFORE ME THIS _____ DAY OF _____ .
19_____ .

DEALER'S NAME (TO AGREE WITH LICENSE)   DEALER CERTIFICATE NO.

MY COMMISSION EXPIRES: _____

BY _____
AUTHORIZED AGENT TO SIGN HERE AFTER ENTERING NAME OF PURCHASER

_____ (SEAL)
SIGNATURE OF NOTARY PUBLIC IN INK

A. ALTERATIONS OR ERASURES WILL VOID THIS TITLE
B. LIEN OR ENCUMBRANCE—ENTER IN OWNER'S APPLICATION FOR TITLE
C. RETAIL PURCHASER MUST APPLY FOR NEW TITLE WITHIN 20 DAYS AFTER PURCHASE OR PAY STATUTORY PENALTY

(Form III) Part A. Assignment of Title by Registered Owner

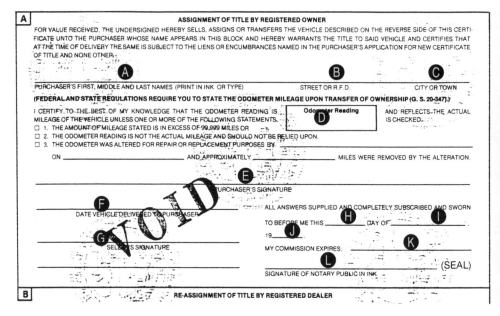

A. Full typed or printed name of purchaser.
B. Purchaser's street or box address.
C. Purchaser's address, city or town.
D. Vehicle's odometer reading on date of assignment of title.
E. Purchaser's full signature.
F. Date vehicle delivered to purchaser (usually date title was assigned).
G. Seller's full signature.

H. Date notary takes certification (notary is certifying only seller's execution).
I. Month notary takes certification.
J. Year notary takes certification.
K. Date, month, and year notary's commission expires.
L. Notary's signature as it appears in the seal or stamp.

(Form III) Part B. Reassignment of Title by Registered Dealer

B RE-ASSIGNMENT OF TITLE BY REGISTERED DEALER

FOR VALUE RECEIVED, THE UNDERSIGNED HEREBY SELLS, ASSIGNS OR TRANSFERS THE VEHICLE DESCRIBED ON THE REVERSE SIDE OF THIS CERTIFICATE UNTO THE PURCHASER WHOSE NAME APPEARS IN THIS BLOCK AND HEREBY WARRANTS THE TITLE TO SAID VEHICLE AND CERTIFIES THAT AT THE TIME OF DELIVERY THE SAME IS SUBJECT TO THE LIENS OR ENCUMBRANCES NAMED IN THE PURCHASER'S APPLICATION FOR NEW CERTIFICATE OF TITLE AND NONE OTHER.

PURCHASER'S FIRST, MIDDLE AND LAST NAMES (PRINT IN INK OR TYPE) STREET OR R.F.D. CITY OR TOWN

(FEDERAL AND STATE REGULATIONS REQUIRE YOU TO STATE THE ODOMETER MILEAGE UPON TRANSFER OF OWNERSHIP (G. S. 20-347).)

I CERTIFY TO THE BEST OF MY KNOWLEDGE THAT THE ODOMETER READING IS | **Odometer Reading** | AND REFLECTS THE ACTUAL MILEAGE OF THE VEHICLE UNLESS ONE OR MORE OF THE FOLLOWING STATEMENTS | | IS CHECKED:

☐ 1. THE AMOUNT OF MILEAGE STATED IS IN EXCESS OF 99,999 MILES, OR

☐ 2. THE ODOMETER READING IS NOT THE ACTUAL MILEAGE AND SHOULD NOT BE RELIED UPON.

☐ 3. THE ODOMETER WAS ALTERED FOR REPAIR OR REPLACEMENT PURPOSES BY

ON _____ AND APPROXIMATELY _____ MILES WERE REMOVED BY THE ALTERATION.

PURCHASER'S SIGNATURE

DATE VEHICLE DELIVERED TO PURCHASER

ALL ANSWERS SUPPLIED AND COMPLETELY SUBSCRIBED AND SWORN

TO BEFORE ME THIS _____ DAY OF _____

19 ___ .

DEALER'S NAME (TO AGREE WITH LICENSE) DEALER CERTIFICATE NO.

MY COMMISSION EXPIRES: _____

BY: _____

AUTHORIZED AGENT TO SIGN HERE AFTER ENTERING NAME OF PURCHASER SIGNATURE OF NOTARY PUBLIC IN INK (SEAL)

A. ALTERATIONS OR ERASURES WILL VOID THIS TITLE
B. LIEN OR ENCUMBRANCE—ENTER IN OWNER'S APPLICATION FOR TITLE
C. RETAIL PURCHASER MUST APPLY FOR NEW TITLE WITHIN 20 DAYS AFTER PURCHASE OR PAY STATUTORY PENALTY

A. Full typed or printed name of purchaser.

B. Purchaser's street or box address.

C. Purchaser's address, city or town.

D. Vehicle's odometer reading on date of reassignment of title.

E. Purchaser's full signature.

F. Date vehicle delivered to purchaser.

G. Full typed or printed name of dealer.

H. Dealer's certificate number.

I. Signature of dealer's agent (omission of this item will cause application to be rejected).

J. Date notary takes certification.

K. Month notary takes certification.

L. Year notary takes certification.

M. Date, month, and year notary's commission expires.

N. Notary's signature as it appears in the seal or stamp.

▼ *Example*: Alec Wilder Stewart sells his 1987 BMW to Hawkins Motor Company. Hawkins then sells the BMW to David Rose French. All of the transactions take place in Charlotte, North Carolina, before different Mecklenburg County notaries.

A

ASSIGNMENT OF TITLE BY REGISTERED OWNER

FOR VALUE RECEIVED, THE UNDERSIGNED HEREBY SELLS, ASSIGNS OR TRANSFERS THE VEHICLE DESCRIBED ON THE REVERSE SIDE OF THIS CERTI-FICATE UNTO THE PURCHASER WHOSE NAME APPEARS IN THIS BLOCK AND HEREBY WARRANTS THE TITLE TO SAID VEHICLE AND CERTIFIES THAT AT THE TIME OF DELIVERY THE SAME IS SUBJECT TO THE LIENS OR ENCUMBRANCES NAMED IN THE PURCHASER'S APPLICATION FOR NEW CERTIFICATE OF TITLE AND NONE OTHER.

Hawkins Motor Company   2 Lions Blvd.   Charlotte

PURCHASER'S FIRST, MIDDLE AND LAST NAMES (PRINT IN INK OR TYPE)   STREET OR R.F.D.   CITY OR TOWN

(FEDERAL AND STATE REGULATIONS REQUIRE YOU TO STATE THE ODOMETER MILEAGE UPON TRANSFER OF OWNERSHIP (G. S. 20-347).)

I CERTIFY TO THE BEST OF MY KNOWLEDGE THAT THE ODOMETER READING IS **Odometer Reading 88049** AND REFLECTS THE ACTUAL MILEAGE OF THE VEHICLE UNLESS ONE OR MORE OF THE FOLLOWING STATEMENTS. IS CHECKED:

☐ 1. THE AMOUNT OF MILEAGE STATED IS IN EXCESS OF 99,999 MILES OR

☐ 2. THE ODOMETER READING IS NOT THE ACTUAL MILEAGE AND SHOULD NOT BE RELIED UPON.

☐ 3. THE ODOMETER WAS ALTERED FOR REPAIR OR REPLACEMENT PURPOSES BY

ON _____ AND APPROXIMATELY _____ MILES WERE REMOVED BY THE ALTERATION.

Hawkins Motor Company by _Jennifer Grayson_   PURCHASER'S SIGNATURE

8/19/91

DATE VEHICLE DELIVERED TO PURCHASER

Alec W. Stewart SELLER'S SIGNATURE

ALL ANSWERS SUPPLIED AND COMPLETELY SUBSCRIBED AND SWORN TO BEFORE ME THIS 19th DAY OF August 19 91

MY COMMISSION EXPIRES: February 5, 1995

Allison Bukterbaum (SEAL)

SIGNATURE OF NOTARY PUBLIC IN INK

B

RE-ASSIGNMENT OF TITLE BY REGISTERED DEALER

FOR VALUE RECEIVED, THE UNDERSIGNED HEREBY SELLS, ASSIGNS OR TRANSFERS THE VEHICLE DESCRIBED ON THE REVERSE SIDE OF THIS CERTI-FICATE UNTO THE PURCHASER WHOSE NAME APPEARS IN THIS BLOCK AND HEREBY WARRANTS THE TITLE TO SAID VEHICLE AND CERTIFIES THAT AT THE TIME OF DELIVERY THE SAME IS SUBJECT TO THE LIENS OR ENCUMBRANCES NAMED IN THE PURCHASER'S APPLICATION FOR NEW CERTIFICATE OF TITLE AND NONE OTHER.

David Rose French   4 Talmage Ct.   Charlotte

PURCHASER'S FIRST, MIDDLE AND LAST NAMES (PRINT IN INK OR TYPE)   STREET OR R.F.D.   CITY OR TOWN

(FEDERAL AND STATE REGULATIONS REQUIRE YOU TO STATE THE ODOMETER MILEAGE UPON TRANSFER OF OWNERSHIP (G. S. 20-347).)

I CERTIFY TO THE BEST OF MY KNOWLEDGE THAT THE ODOMETER READING IS **Odometer Reading 88049** AND REFLECTS THE ACTUAL MILEAGE OF THE VEHICLE UNLESS ONE OR MORE OF THE FOLLOWING STATEMENTS IS CHECKED:

☐ 1. THE AMOUNT OF MILEAGE STATED IS IN EXCESS OF 99,999 MILES OR

☐ 2. THE ODOMETER READING IS NOT THE ACTUAL MILEAGE AND SHOULD NOT BE RELIED UPON.

☐ 3. THE ODOMETER WAS ALTERED FOR REPAIR OR REPLACEMENT PURPOSES BY

ON _____ AND APPROXIMATELY _____ MILES WERE REMOVED BY THE ALTERATION.

David Rose French PURCHASER'S SIGNATURE

8/20/91

DATE VEHICLE DELIVERED TO PURCHASER

Hawkins Motor Company 8116 DEALER'S NAME (TO AGREE WITH LICENSE)   DEALER CERTIFICATE NO.

BY: _Lisa Xavier Stephens_ AUTHORIZED AGENT TO SIGN HERE AFTER ENTERING NAME OF PURCHASER

ALL ANSWERS SUPPLIED AND COMPLETELY SUBSCRIBED AND SWORN TO BEFORE ME THIS 20th DAY OF August 19 91

MY COMMISSION EXPIRES: 3/31/93

Mary Jass Stewart (SEAL)

SIGNATURE OF NOTARY PUBLIC IN INK

A. ALTERATIONS OR ERASURES WILL VOID THIS TITLE

B. LIEN OR ENCUMBRANCE—ENTER IN OWNER'S APPLICATION FOR TITLE

C. RETAIL PURCHASER MUST APPLY FOR NEW TITLE WITHIN 20 DAYS AFTER PURCHASE OR PAY STATUTORY PENALTY

▼ Form IV

Form IV is the application-for-title form that must be used when the former owner has assigned his or her title by means of Form III. The form is rather complicated, and if the person who appears before the notary to certify execution of the application has difficulty completing the form or has

MVR-1
(Rev. 9/89)

NORTH CAROLINA DIVISION OF MOTOR VEHICLES
TITLE APPLICATION

Plate Expires _____

Plate Valid Thru _____

Title Suffix

FOR DMV USE ONLY

Date

Year	Make	Body Style	Series Model	Title Number _____		
				Plate #	License	
Vehicle Identification Number			Type of Fuel		MSI	
				Sticker #	Title	
					Special Title	
Full Name(s) of Owner(s) (First, Middle, Last) (Print in Ink or Type)			Check When ☐ One Name ☐ Initial Only		Registration	
				Classification	Late Pen./Misc.	
			Check When ☐ One Name ☐ Initial Only		Use Tax	
				Gross Weight	Lien Rec.	
Residence Address (Individual) Business Address (Firm)			Property Tax Declaration		Rest.	
				Annual Fee	Service	
City and State		Zip Code	County		Per/Spec./Desi.	
					Pen (overwt.)	
Mail Address (if different from above)			Municipality	Branch #/Agent		
					Sub Total	
					Notary	
				Date/Time		
					Total	

OWNER'S CERTIFICATION FOR ELIGIBILITY

I CERTIFY FOR THE MOTOR VEHICLE DESCRIBED ABOVE THAT:

1. I have financial responsibility as required by law.

Print or type full name of insurance company licensed in N.C.—not agency or group

Policy Number—if policy not issued, name of agent binding coverage

2. I owe no delinquent county or municipal taxes on this vehicle.
3. I was the legal owner of this vehicle on January 1st of the year of this application and the vehicle was listed for property taxes

in _____ (County) in _____ (Month) _____ (Year)

4. I was not the legal owner of this vehicle on January 1st of the year of this application. ☐ (CHECK BLOCK)

Check Appropriate Block/s

☐ Title Only—Vehicle Not in Operation.

☐ Title and License

☐ Exchanged Plate No. _____

☐ Plate No. Transferred _____

Sticker No. _____

Expiration Date _____

☐ Replaced Plate No. _____

DMV VALIDATION

ODOMETER READING

FIRST LIEN		Date of Lien	**SECOND LIEN**		Date of Lien
Lienholder			Lienholder		
Address			Address		
City	State	Zip Code	City	State	Zip Code

Date First Operated in N.C.	State of Last Registration	Passenger Capacity	N.C. Dealer No.	Empty Weight	Combined Gross Weight of Truck or Truck-Tractor with Trailer

Purchased ☐ New ☐ Used	SALES PRICE	Purchased for Use in N.C. ☐ Yes ☐ No	From Whom Purchased (Name and Address)		Purchase Date

Is This Vehicle Leased? ☐ Yes ☐ No   Check Block/s Indicating Change or Alteration of   Class of License

If Yes, Attach Form 330 or Lease Agreement   ☐ Motor ☐ Body ☐ Identification No.   (Attach Explanation)

I (we) am (are) the owner(s) of the vehicle described on this application and request that a North Carolina Certificate of Title be issued. I (we) certify that the information on the application is correct to the best of my (our) knowledge. The vehicle is subject to the liens named and no others. If a registration plate is issued or transferred, I (we) further certify that there has not been a registration plate revocation and that liability insurance is in effect on this vehicle on the date of this application as required by the North Carolina Financial Security Act of 1957.

OWNER'S SIGNATURE: _____

First Name   Middle Name   Last Name

Application must be signed in ink by each owner or authorized representative of firms or corporations.

ACKNOWLEDGMENT	**DMV USE ONLY**

Subscribed and sworn to before me this _____ day of _____

19 _____ .

Notary Public _____

(SEAL)   Address _____

My Commission Expires _____

questions about it, the notary should refer him or her to the nearest motor vehicle registration office (the notary should do this any time a person has difficulty completing a title document). The notary is concerned only with the owner/applicant's signature and the acknowledgment.

▼ *Example (continuing the example from Form III)*: When David Rose French applies for a title to the 1987 BMW in his name, he will use Form IV. When he appears before a notary to acknowledge execution of the application, it will be taken as follows:

4. I was not the legal owner of this vehicle on January 1st of the year of this application. ☐ (CHECK BLOCK)			☐ **Replaced Plate No.** _____		ODOMETER READING		
FIRST LIEN		Date of Lien	**SECOND LIEN**			Date of Lien	
Lienholder Automobile Finance Corp.			Lienholder				
Address 822 Warren St.			Address				
City Charlotte	State N.C.	Zip Code 28046	City		State	Zip Code	
Date First Operated in N.C. 8/20/91	State of Last Registration NC	Passenger Capacity 5	N.C. Dealer No.	Empty Weight 4550	Combined Gross Weight of Truck or Truck-Tractor with Trailer		
Purchased ☐ New ☒ Used	SALES PRICE 16,850	Purchased for Use in N.C. ☒ Yes ☐ No	From Whom Purchased (Name and Address) Hawkins Motor Co.				Purchase Date 8/20/91
Is This Vehicle Leased? ☐ Yes ☒ No		Check Block/s Indicating Change or Alteration of				Class of License	
If Yes, Attach Form 330 or Lease Agreement		☐ Motor ☐ Body ☐ Identification No.		(Attach Explanation)		D	

I (we) am (are) the owner(s) of the vehicle described on this application and request that a North Carolina Certificate of Title be issued. I (we) certify that the information on the application is correct to the best of my (our) knowledge. The vehicle is subject to the liens named and no others. If a registration plate is issued or transferred, I (we) further certify that there has not been a registration plate revocation and that liability insurance is in effect on this vehicle on the date of this application as required by the North Carolina Financial Security Act of 1957.

OWNER'S SIGNATURE: *David ___ Rose ___ French*
First Name   Middle Name   Last Name

Application must be signed in ink by each owner or authorized representative of firms or corporations.

ACKNOWLEDGMENT	DMV USE ONLY
Subscribed and sworn to before me this 24th day of August 19 91. (SEAL) Notary Public *Daniel Brady* Address 17 Rue de Rivoli, Charlotte, NC My Commission Expires 4/1/94	

V
Oaths

Whenever the notarial certificate contains the words "sworn to" or "duly sworn," the notary public must administer an oath to the person whose acknowledgment or proof is being taken. (In the following discussion, the word "oath" should be understood to include "affirmation," which is a solemn pledge or declaration and may be used in place of an oath by any person who prefers not to take an oath—see below.) A notary should *always* administer an oath when the attestation certificate calls for one.

Notary's Authority

Under North Carolina law, a notary public may administer any oath, including an oath of office, except when the law requires that another official administer the particular oath.[1] For example, a notary may not administer the oath of office to another notary, because a statute specifically provides that notaries must take this oath before a register of deeds.[2] Whenever the law prescribes an oath without specifying the officer before whom it must be taken, a notary may administer the oath.

Under federal law, a North Carolina notary acting within North Carolina may administer any oath authorized or required under the laws of the United States,[3] including oaths of office for all federal offices.[4] In addition to this general authorization, notaries are specifically authorized to take oaths of office for national-bank directors[5] and oaths with respect to adverse claims of mining rights.[6]

---

1. N.C. Gen. Stat. §§ 10A-9(a)(2), 11-7.1(a)(3).
2. *Id.* § 10.2.
3. 5 U.S.C. § 2903(c)(2).
4. *Id.* § 2903(a).
5. 12 U.S.C. § 73.
6. 30 U.S.C. § 31.

Procedure

A person taking an oath should place one hand on the Holy Scriptures.[7] This book will vary depending on the person's religious beliefs: Christians should use the New Testament or the Bible; Jews, the Torah or the Old Testament; Moslems, the Koran; Hindus, the Bhagavad-Gita; etc.

A person who affirms rather than swears should use the same words as the oath, except that he or she should say "affirm" rather than "swear" and should omit the words "so help me, God."[8] A person being affirmed is not required to place his or her hand on any book or document.

All oaths of office and many other oaths must be subscribed by the person who gives the oath and then filed in a particular place.[9] If the oath does not appear on a printed form, the proper procedure is to type out the text, administer it to the person, have him or her sign it, and attest it in the following fashion:[10]

```
Sworn to and subscribed before me this _____ day
of _____, 19___.

(Official Seal)                    _____
                                        Notary Public

My commission expires _____, 19___.
```

The person being sworn is responsible for filing the subscribed and attested oath in the proper office.

Oaths of Office

All persons elected or appointed to public office in this state must take an oath to support the constitutions of the United States and North Carolina.[11] The constitutional oath is as follows:

I, _____, do solemnly swear [or affirm] that I will support and maintain the Constitution and laws of the

---

7. *Id.* § 11-2.
8. *Id.* § 11-4.
9. *See id.,* § 14-229, and N.C. CONST. art. VI, § 7.
10. This form of acknowledgment is known as a jurat.
11. N.C. CONST. art. VI, § 7.

United States, and the Constitution and laws of North Carolina not inconsistent therewith, and that I will faithfully discharge the duties of my office as _____, so help me, God.

These persons are also required by G.S. 11-7 to take the following oath:

I, _____, do solemnly swear that I will support the Constitution of the United States; that I will be faithful and bear true allegiance to the State of North Carolina, and to the constitutional powers and authorities which are or may be established for government thereof; and that I will endeavor to support, maintain, and defend the Constitution of said State, not inconsistent with the Constitution of the United States, to the best of my knowledge and ability, so help me, God.

Oaths of Corporations

The oath of a corporation is given by and through an officer or agent of the corporation authorized by law to verify pleadings on behalf of the corporation.[12] The interested parties are responsible for seeing that the appropriate officer appears before the notary to take an oath for a corporation.

---

12. N.C. Gen. Stat. § 11-5.

VI
Affidavits

An affidavit is a voluntary statement in writing sworn to or affirmed as true before an officer authorized to administer oaths.[1] The purpose of an affidavit is "to obtain the sworn statement of facts . . . of the affiant [the person making the affidavit] in such official and authoritative shape, as that it may be used for any lawful purposes, either in or out of courts of justice."[2] Unlike depositions, which are usually compelled and taken only after notice to all parties to a lawsuit, affidavits are voluntary statements used in a wide variety of governmental and business affairs—as evidence of, for example, a person's age, the title to property, the pedigree of animals, and the financial condition of a loan applicant.

Notary's Authority

A North Carolina notary public acting within North Carolina may take affidavits[3] except when the law prescribes another official before whom a specific affidavit must be sworn. Thus an insolvent debtor's affidavit for assignment of his estate for the benefit of creditors may be taken only by a clerk of the superior court.[4] Also, a notary may not take his own affidavit, since he may not administer an oath to himself.

Like North Carolina law, federal law allows affidavits to be used in many ways. Because a North Carolina notary acting within North Carolina may administer oaths under federal law,[5] he may also take affidavits under federal law except for specific affidavits that must be taken by another designated official.

---

1. BLACK'S LAW DICTIONARY 80 (4th ed. 1951).
2. Alford v. McCormac, 90 N.C. 151, 153 (1884).
3. N.C. GEN. STAT. § 10A-9(a)(2).
4. *Id.* § 23-13.
5. 5 U.S.C. § 2903(c)(2).

Components

An affidavit has the following components:

Caption. An affidavit for a legal proceeding should include a caption that recites the county and state in which the action is pending, the names of the parties, the name of the court, and the label "Affidavit." Other affidavits should include a title briefly describing the nature of the matter and naming the county and state in which the affidavit was given.

Preamble. The preamble follows the caption and is simply a statement that the named person appeared before the notary, was duly sworn, and made the following affidavit. Although not essential to an affidavit's validity, the preamble is usually included for introductory purposes.

Allegations. The statements of the affiant follow the preamble, usually in numbered paragraphs, each paragraph containing only one allegation. The first allegation should always state the affiant's relationship to the action or to the parties.

Affiant's Signature. Although the absence of his signature does not technically invalidate an affidavit,[6] the affiant should sign his name below the allegations. Omission of a signature raises doubts about the affidavit's validity and may invalidate it in other states.

Jurat. The jurat, or notary's certificate that the affidavit was subscribed and sworn to (or affirmed) at a specified time and place, appears after the affiant's signature. The jurat should be attested by a notary in the usual manner.

Procedure

Although a statement may be reduced to writing in a notary's presence when it is sworn to or affirmed, it is usually already in writing when brought before the notary. In either case, the notary should administer the following oath according to the procedure described in Chapter V:

> Do you swear [or affirm] that the statements contained in this writing are the truth, by your own knowledge or by your information and belief, so help you, God?

After taking the oath, the affiant signs the affidavit or identifies an earlier signature as his own, and the notary adds his certificate (jurat) and

---

6. Alford v. McCormac, 90 N.C. 151 (1884).

attestation. "Subscribed and sworn to [or affirmed] before me this _____ day of _____, 19___" is sufficient.

Preparing an affidavit sufficient to accomplish the desired result is the responsibility of the party and his attorney. The notary's duties are, first, to ensure that the affiant is who he claims to be (persons not known to the notary should be asked to identify themselves appropriately) and swears to the truthfulness of the statements in the affidavit, and, second, to certify the affidavit properly.

Facts that belong in the body of the affidavit ought not to be included in the preamble. For example, an affidavit that begins with "John Doe, President of X.Y.Z. Corporation, being duly sworn, says . . ." is incorrect. The fact that John Doe is president of X.Y.Z. Corporation should appear in the first allegation, not in the preamble.

Verification of Pleadings

In some kinds of lawsuits—such as divorce,[7] habeas corpus,[8] or certain suits by shareholders or members of a corporation or unincorporated association[9]—the parties or their attorneys must verify the pleadings (complaints filed by the plaintiff and answers filed by the defendant); this is done by executing an affidavit of verification according to Rule 11 of the North Carolina Rules of Civil Procedure. The content of the affidavit varies according to the type of lawsuit, and the party seeking the affidavit and his or her attorney are responsible for preparing it correctly. The notary's responsibilities are to administer an oath and to complete the jurat, or certification, correctly.

Forms

The two basic forms for affidavits—one for private matters, the other for legal proceedings—are below. Many affidavits are available on printed forms; others may be found in R. Simms, *The North Carolina Manual of Law and Forms* (10th ed. 1951); L. Douglas, *Forms* (2d ed. 1953); E. John, *American Notaries* (6th ed. 1951). See also W. Sheffield III, *North Carolina Practice, Civil Procedure Forms*, Ch. 9 (1981).

---

7. N.C. Gen. Stat. § 50-8.
8. *Id.* § 17-7(5).
9. N.C. R. Civ. P. 23(b).

▼   **Private matters**

The following form is the general affidavit for use between private parties, not in legal proceedings. The components of an affidavit (discussed above) are indicated by marginal notes.

[Caption or title] ▶

North Carolina

Affidavit

_____ County

[Preamble] ▶

_____, appearing before the undersigned notary and being duly sworn, says that:

[Allegations] ▶

Set out title or position, residence, and relationship to the parties or the matter for which the affidavit is desired.

Set out declarations of affiant in numbered paragraphs.

1. He is _____
   _____
   _____
   _____
   _____

2. _____
   _____
   _____

[Affiant's signature] ▶

_____
Affiant

Sworn to (or affirmed) and subscribed before me this _____ day of _____ _____, 19___.

[Jurat] ▶

Official Seal
Notary Public

My commission expires _____, 19___.

Note: The following preamble may be used instead of the one above:

_____ personally appeared before me in _____ , _____ County, State of _____, and having been duly sworn (or affirmed), according to law, made the following affidavit, to wit: . . .

▼ Legal proceedings

The following is usual form of an affidavit for a court or other legal proceeding. The components of such an affidavit (discussed above) are indicated by marginal notes.

[Venue] ▶

North Carolina   General Court of Justice
_____ Court Division
_____County

_____

[Caption or title] ▶

Plaintiff(s)
vs.   Affidavit

_____

Defendant(s)

[Preamble] ▶

_____, appearing before the undersigned notary and being duly sworn, says that:

[Allegations] ▶

Set out title or position, residence, and relationship to the parties or the matter for which the affidavit is desired.

1. He is _____
   _____
   _____
   _____
   _____
   _____

Set out declarations of affiant in numbered paragraphs.

2. _____
   _____
   _____

[Affiant's signature] ▶

_____
                                    Affiant

Sworn to (or affirmed) and subscribed before me this _____ day of _____ _____, 19___.

[Jurat] ▶

(Official Seal)
Notary Public

My commission expires _____, 19___.